The World of Hummingbirds

An Illustrated Guide to these Marvels of Nature

The World of Hummingbirds

An Illustrated Guide to these Marvels of Nature

Tony Tilford

GRAMERCY BOOKS
NEW YORK

Acknowledgements

I would like to thank those who have assisted me in the preparation of this book in particular my son Robert Tilford, Dr John Cooke, Ivor Grogan, Ali Daghir, John Goldsmith, and Roy and Gail Edmonds.

Hummingbird photography can be fraught with difficulties often requiring long and arduous journeys and in difficult weather conditions. My special thanks, therefore, go out to the many photographers who have provided such an excellent collection of photographs.

Page ii: **A Giant Hummingbird (*Patagona gigas*) nest on a cactus in Peru.**

This 2000 edition is published by Gramercy Books™,
an imprint of Random House Value Publishing, Inc.,
280 Park Avenue, New York, NY 10017,
by arrangement with PRC Publishing Ltd,
Kiln House, 210 New Kings Road, London, SW6 4NZ.

Printed and bound in China

Random House
New York • Toronto • London • Sydney • Auckland
http://www.randomhouse.com/

A catalogue record for this book is available from the Library of Congress.

ISBN 0-517-16170-2

8 7 6 5 4 3 2 1

Contents

Part 1: Introduction 6

Jewels in Flight 6

Hummingbirds and Humans 8

Evolution 10

Biology 10

Plumage 13

Feeding 16

Artificial Feeding and Gardening for Hummingbirds 20

Hummingbirds' Symbiosis with Flowering Plants. 22

Behavior 23

Breeding 25

Distribution, Migration, and Movements 28

Scientific Study of Hummingbirds 30

Part 2: A Gallery of Hummingbirds 32

Part 3: Reference

A Checklist of the Hummingbirds of the World 144

Hummingbird Hotspots 152

Useful Web Sites 153

Bibliography & Further Reading 155

Index 157

Introduction

Jewels in Flight

Right: **In certain light, the iridescent plumage of the Ruby Topaz Hummingbird (*Chrysolampis mosquitus*) shines like a brilliant, deep ruby.**

Below: **This male Purple-crowned Woodnymph (*Thalurania colombica venusta*) from the rain forests of Costa Rica has incredibly iridescent plumage that reflects the rays of sunlight as they break through the dark tree canopy.**

Although this simple title has been used by others, I cannot find a better description and it seems neither can those who have bestowed the common names on a large proportion of the hummingbirds. Emerald, sapphire, ruby, azure, garnet, amethyst, tourmaline, and topaz are just a few jewels; and all these names of brightly colored, precious gems have also been used to describe the beautiful iridescent colors of hummingbirds. Reading through the Checklist of Hummingbirds at the back of this book, one can be easily forgiven for mistaking it as a catalog of gemstones and precious metals.

But it goes further than that, with many evocative names such as woodnymph, scintillant, brilliant, and mountain-gem also being used, while other names, such as coquette, streamertail, puffleg, plumeleteer, visorbearer, and spatuletail, seem more reminiscent of a carnival. Of course, there are many hummingbirds with more descriptive names such as awlbill, sabrewing, plovercrest, coronet, firecrown, and thornbill and then there are those that describe their origin such as Carib, Inca, and Hillstar. Even the more subdued brown, red, and grayish colored group identified as the Hermits have a name that not only describes their often reclusive nature but the duller coloration associated with a being living in solitude. The scientific names are similarly inclined to be beautifully descriptive but that must be expected for such a fascinating and lovely family of birds.

Hummingbirds and Humans

The family name of hummingbird has obviously derived from the sound caused by the very fast beat of their wings. With the fastest wingbeat, approaching 200 beats per second, the hummingbirds' wings move so rapidly that they cannot be seen by the human eye, but the low-pitched hum is audible for those close enough to hear.

Humans have forever been fascinated by hummingbirds and have generally treated them with respect. They pose no threat to our livelihood in any way and are treated as elements of beauty, giving pleasure wherever they are seen. However, they have been persecuted in the past. Historically, and even to the present, native peoples of South America have used them as embellishments for their dress. Iridescent feathers and, often, whole skins were used by the Aztecs and Mayans to adorn their ceremonial dress. The Incas and Nazcas of the Andes also held the hummingbird in very high esteem and the huge figures carved into the desert plateaux of Peru are thought to be depictions of hummingbirds. In Victorian times, hummingbirds were collected for the taxidermy trade and huge collections set up under glass domes can still be seen in many museums around the world. Toward the end of the 19th century, millions of hummingbird skins were also imported into Europe for the millinery and fashion trade. Sadly the beauty of their iridescent plumage has now all but disappeared.

There is still a small trade in live hummingbirds for the birdkeeping enthusiast but most are now well protected. The trade is strictly regulated by the Washington Convention on International Trade in Endangered Species (CITES) due to the continued concern for the status of most of the species. All hummingbirds are covered by these international laws and most countries strictly adhere to them. Fortunately many of the birds now exported are going to very dedicated birdkeepers who are at last gaining the knowledge and experience to breed them in captivity. Captive breeding success has been poor in the past, but given the right conditions and species knowledge as well as the availability of specially formulated foods, there is no reason why greater success should not be achieved in the future. The benefit of keeping these lovely creatures in captivity is that successful breeding may eventually be a useful conservation tool in saving endangered species.

Below: **This recently fledged hummingbird has been bred in captivity in England.**

Currently the most threatened species of hummingbird is thought to be the Hook-billed Hermit (*Glaucis dohrnii*) from eastern Brazil. Only about 50 are estimated to exist, but as the population is drastically fragmented and difficult to count there could be more. They are a lowland forest-dwelling species and their habitat is under enormous pressure from human intrusion and destruction. With the huge expansion of towns, roads, industry, and agriculture, as well as logging and mining, conservation measures stand little chance against human onslaught.

Other highly endangered species include the Honduran Emerald (*Polyerata luciae*), Juan Fernandez Firecrown (*Sephanoides fernandensis*), Scissor-tailed Hummingbird (*Hylonympha macrocerca*), Sapphire-bellied Hummingbird (*Lepidopyga lilliae*), and the Black-breasted Puffleg (*Eriocnemis nigrivestis*). As would be expected, the main threat to all of these very rare species is humankind's slow but persistent destruction of their habitat. The Turquoise-throated Puffleg (*Eriocnemis godini*), an endemic species from northern Ecuador, is currently known only from museum specimens and thought to be extinct, its forest habitat having been completely destroyed.

Below: **These lines on the desert plateau in Peru are thought to depict a hummingbird.**

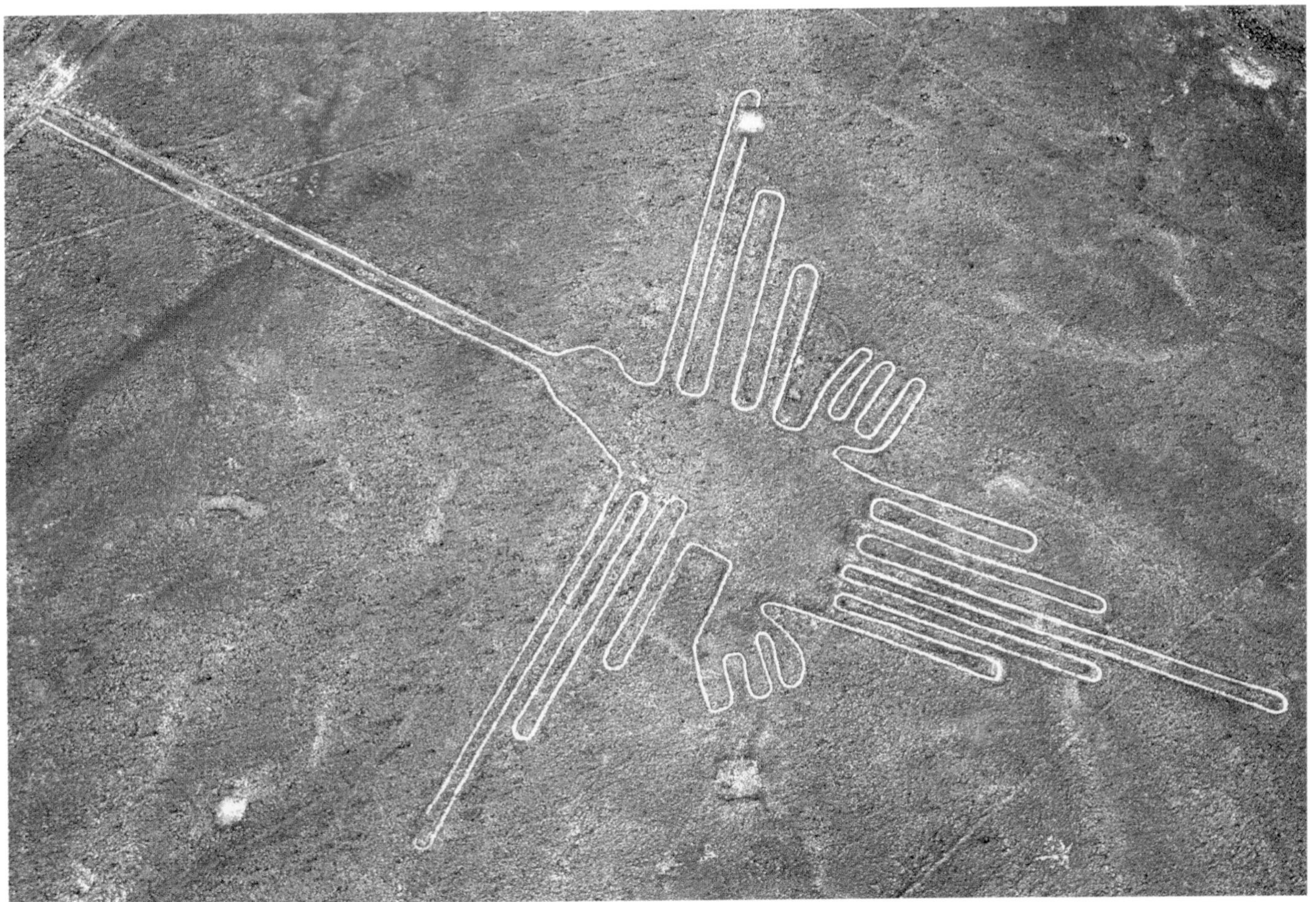

Evolution

Hummingbirds are thought to be closely related to the swifts (Apodidae) and treeswifts (Hemiprocnidae); more because of their anatomical and morphological similarities. It is unknown whether they have common ancestry or whether the two avian forms have become similar, but it may not be coincidence that the two share some unique elements of body chemistry. Perhaps they were at one time alike and a divergence of form commenced many millions of years ago. There are theories that this may have occurred when the tectonic plate on which South America presently stands broke away from Gondwanaland (the ancient supercontinent), but only in time may science discover the true relationships.

Biology

The likeness of the swifts and hummingbirds is based upon the similarities of neck musculature and the way nerves are supplied to the wing muscles as well as the more familiar comparison of the skeleton associated with flight.

Hummingbirds stand apart in their adaptation to hovering flight, which appears well designed to exploit nectar from flowering plants. The skeleton has adapted in unique ways to allow the wings to move differently to other avian forms. Hummingbirds depend entirely on very powerful flight muscles and the suitable skeleton to which they are attached. Not only do they have a proportionally longer and deeper sternum; they have eight pairs of ribs compared to the six of most other bird families. To allow flexibility of the wing as it moves through almost 180 degrees of movement, the sternum has acquired a shallow depression at its junction with the powerful coracoid bones. This acts as a socket for the ball-shaped end of the short wing bone (humerus) much like a conventional mechanical ball and socket joint. The wing bones, equivalent to the humerus, radius, and ulna of the human arm, are much shorter than those adapted for conventional avian flight and they terminate at another series of bones which support the ten main flight feathers. These bones, comparative to the bones of the hand, are proportionally much longer. Unlike other small birds, hummingbirds have only six or seven secondary wing feathers instead of the customary nine. In general, the ten primary flight feathers decrease in size from the long outer feathers inward towards the secondaries; however, a few species differ from this rule.

The combination of these mechanical factors has led to a very adaptable flight machine more comparable to the helicopter. So much so that

Above: **Hummingbirds are capable of rapid straight flight as can be seen by this Green Violet-ear (*Colibri thalassinus*).**

they have the ability not only to hover but also to fly forward, backward, and occasionally even upside down.

The advantages of this mechanical design allow lift to be achieved on both forward and return wing strokes of the figure of eight pattern of movement undertaken during hovering flight. On the forward stroke the pressure of air causing lift is on the bottom surface of the wing feathers, but as they are rotated through 90 degrees for the return, the pressure changes to what is normally the top surface and now facing down, once again generating lift. The bird can therefore hold its position in the air with just a balancing control from the tail.

So much emphasis is put on the hovering ability of the hummingbirds that normal forward flight is frequently forgotten. They are remarkably good at flying and indeed for the long distance migrations performed by some species it is absolutely essential. However, like helicopters, most do not have the endurance that more conventional flying machines possess. They need to refuel more frequently and long distances are often covered in a series of short journeys. The exceptions to this pattern are those few North American migrants which accumulate deposits of fat to enable them to cover long distances without refueling.

Above: **A Purple-throated Mountain Gem (*Lampornis castaneoventris calolaema*) hovering at an epiphytic bromeliad (*Tillandsia insignis*).**

Their routine flight pattern seems to consist mainly of bouts of hovering flight at feeding stations interspersed with fairly fast, straight forward dashes in between. Scientific study with hummingbirds in wind tunnels has established flying speeds of between 30 and 50 miles per hour (50-80km/hour), but in the wild some species are known to get up to 60 miles per hour (100km/hour). In bouts of chasing it is estimated that speeds approaching 100 miles per hour (160km/hour) can be achieved.

The muscle mass responsible for this specialized flight adaptation accounts for 30 per cent of the total body mass, approximately 50 per cent more than any other strong-flying bird. These muscles demand large volumes of oxygen, especially when hovering, and consequently the heart is also of proportionately larger size. The heart normally beats at 500 to 600 times a minute but can achieve almost 1,000 beats per minute when exceptionally fast responses are required.

The close association of hummingbirds with the swifts has been linked in part to their likeness in neck musculature. It is thought that the special arrangement of the bird's neck allows particularly fast responses of head movement, particularly from side to side, while catching aerial insects in high-speed flight.

Left: **The somber plumage of this female Broad-tailed Hummingbird (*Selasphorus platycercus*) and her young is very important camouflage during breeding.**

Plumage

As with most other species, plumage coloration is closely associated with behavior. Some birds need to display their characteristics while others need to hide them.

Quite obviously, breeding females and immature birds need to remain more concealed as they are particularly vulnerable to predators, whereas males generally need to stand out, particularly if they are polygamous as are hummingbirds. Not only do males use their iridescent plumage to attract partners but also in territorial defense, posturing against other males irrespective of species. The difference in plumage between the sexes is more pronounced in species of more open habitats; but in those of more closed and frequently darker environments such as forests, the iridescence of the males is sometimes absent altogether.

The feathers of adult hummingbirds are most interesting in that they lack the downy underlay present in other species and there are considerably fewer of them. Although a few downy feathers are present while the chick is in the nest, these are soon shed after fledging. This is thought to be an adaptation that has become necessary to dissipate the large amount of heat generated within the body by the hummingbirds vigorous flight activity.

Right: **Adult hummingbirds lack the downy underlay to their plumage and they have fewer feathers.**

The iridescence of hummingbird feathers, particularly visible on the gorgets (throat feathers) and crest plumage of the males, is caused by the physical structure of the feathers. Feather barbules (small barbs fringing the feather) contain layers of minute platelets (very thin melanin structures containing air sacs) each acting as a light interference medium, refracting light waves to produce different colored lighting effects. Within the platelets the melanin is often pigmented, which also has an effect on the colors produced. Depending on the angle of light reflecting from the feather, it may vary considerably from intensely brilliant to not being present at all.

Like most other birds, the pigmented color of the primary and secondary wing feathers gives them their generally dull appearance. In fact most hummingbirds wings appear a very similar color of dark brown to black with infrequent tinged variations.

Only very occasionally, such as in the Purple-throated Carib (*Eulampis jugularis*), do the feathers have an iridescent sheen and in some species the wing coverts are brightly iridescent. These characteristics are undoubtedly due to the feather structure and the need for a strong and durable flight membrane. The flight feathers have small hooked barbules so that they can attach to their adjacent member and provide a cohesive membrane. Generally though, the small, highly-reflective platelets are no advantage in this type of structure and are generally missing and hence the wings have a dull appearance.

The tails of hummingbirds vary considerably in shape and size from the short, straight cut of many species to the long and very elaborate extensions of some such as the Marvelous Spatuletail (*Loddigesia mirabilis*): however, almost all have ten tail feathers except for four in the Marvelous Spatuletail. With so many variations in shape and size, the differences are thought to have occurred through the birds' adaptation to situations of habitat and behavior.

Left: **The gorget feathers of male hummingbirds are often highly iridescent.**

Left: **Hummingbirds flight feathers are usually dark and dull due to their different structure.**

Feeding

Hummingbirds are invariably nectivores, most often seen hovering at the flowers from which they extract nectar along with a little pollen.

Nectar is a necessary food source providing the essential and easily convertible energy demanded by their mode of flight. To maintain their energy requirements, hummingbirds drink several times their body weight of nectar each day and in the process may visit up to around 1,000 flowers. Their long, hollow, and extensible tongues are forked at the tip, each half of the split tip being channel-shaped. Nectar is taken from the flowers into these channels by capillary action but is also assisted by a rapid licking motion. The bill serves not only as a guide for the long tongue, but also as a mechanism for squeezing the nectar back into the digestive system of the body. Regular feeding at around ten minute intervals is essential for most species to maintain their energy requirements. In between the birds go into a state of torpor to allow the food time to digest. Besides the familiar hovering flight used by hummingbirds to get access to flowers, many also get to their food plant by perching on nearby plants or even hanging from them while maintaining their balance by beating their wings in semi-flight.

For most hummingbird species, insects and spiders make up as much as ten per cent of the hummingbird's food intake providing much of the bird's essential protein requirements. Several methods are used to catch insects, but in individuals the system used is generally determined by the bird's bill shape. Species having long bills are more suited to hover-gleaning insects and spiders from foliage, whereas short-billed species are better adapted to hawking flies and wasps. Species in between can frequently be observed using both catching methods.

The bird's bill shape also plays an important part in the efficiency with which nectar can be extracted from flowers. The great variation in shape among hummingbirds' bills determines which flowers they can exploit. For instance, long tubular flowers require a long and often decurved bill for access, while short-billed species are more suited to less deep blooms unless, like several species, they pierce the base of the flower or use holes already pierced by species such as the Bananaquit (*Coereba flaveola*) or flowerpeckers.

Above left: **This female Giant Hummingbird (*Patagona gigas*) still has pollen on her bill from a recent feed.**

Above middle: **This Black-chinned Hummingbird (*Archilochus alexandri*) is showing its long extensible tongue.**

Above right: **This Green Mango (*Anthracothorax viridis*) from Peru has adopted the typical pose of a hummingbird in torpor.**

Left: **A Green-backed Firecrown (*Sephanoides s.*) perched on a nearby twig to get access to the flowers.**

Left: **White-throated Mountain Gem (*Lampornis c. castaneoventris*) foraging for insects.**

Right: **The Sword-billed Hummingbird (*Ensifera ensifera*) is well adapted to take nectar from long bell-shaped flowers.**

Below: **Short-billed hummingbirds frequently use the holes pierced by the Bananaquit (*Coereba flaveola*) to reach the nectar.**

At times of food shortage such as during migration and when flowers are scarce, hummingbirds will resort to other food sources. The sweet sap oozing from trees damaged by woodpeckers, in particular the Sapsuckers (*Sphyrapicus spp.*), is frequently exploited by migrating hummingbirds to North America as they arrive early on their breeding grounds. This attraction is a valuable source of nourishment, not only for its sugary content but also because it attracts many insects upon which the birds can also feed. Similarly hummingbirds are known to consume the sugary excretions deposited by insects.

Whereas many of the smaller species tend to have feeding territories confined to a relatively small group of abundantly flowering shrubs or trees, others depend on "trap-lining," the process of visiting widely distributed suitable flowers in a regular and often set pattern. There are others which behave more generally and adopt both procedures, but because of their intermediate size are able to ignore the threats of the more territorial birds.

The energy required to support the high level of hummingbird activity is proportionally immense and it is understandable that this group of birds has the highest metabolic rate per unit of body weight in the avian world. Their digestive system must ensure rapid conversion of food into energy so its specialized adaptation allows nectar to pass directly from the crop into the small intestine, missing the stomach altogether. Within a short time span of around 15 minutes it is completely digested. On the other hand, solid food passes from the crop into the first section of the stomach where protein is digested by acids and enzymes. From there it continues to be digested in the second and smaller part of the stomach before being passed into the small intestine.

Above: **A Ruby-throated Hummingbird (*Archilochus colubris*) excreting surplus fluid.**

Below: **An Andean Hillstar (*Oreotrochilus estella*) on a bromeliad after dusk.**

It is estimated that hummingbirds consume over one and a half times their bodyweight in fluids and nectar each day, of which much is excreted as urine. This can often be observed at feeders as fluid is passed in a jet from the bird's vent. Could this be another reason why these birds have been known as "rainbirds?"

Energy needs demand that hummingbirds have a regular intake of nectar when they are active, which even extends into dusk and before dawn. Fortunately many have good night vision and are not wholly diurnal as would be expected. This is especially so with some of the high-altitude species who may have extra demands on their metabolism in colder climes.

Artificial Feeding and Gardening for Hummingbirds

It is normal for only part of the hummingbird's essential diet to be provided by artificial feeding—that is the replacement for nectar usually obtained from flowers. So hummingbirds can be attracted to artificial feeding stations but they must also be able to forage for insects and flies. They will come to feeders and accept the easy-to-obtain man-made nectar replacements but will naturally wander around seeking the essential protein provided by insect food. Birds kept in captivity either because they are sick or injured or for conservation and study must always be provided with ample amounts of live food in the form of fruit-flies and the like as well as "nectar foods."

Attracting wild hummingbirds to feeders is an extremely enjoyable pastime for all and certainly boosts the population where natural nectar is in short supply. In many parts of the United States, the population of hummingbirds is way above the level at which natural nectar supplies would support. These "hummingbird hotspots" are usually around feeding stations set up specially to study the birds and they give enormous enjoyment to all those present in the vicinity.

There are numerous proprietary feeders on the market as well as ready prepared "nectar" mixes that need the addition of boiling water. Most of the food mixes are simply sugar with a little coloring and an additive to prevent fermentation. The addition of coloring has no advantage whatsoever as it is the strength of the nectar only which attracts the birds. If it is too weak or too strong, they may prefer to forage elsewhere. It is by far cheaper to prepare simple sugar water solutions and replace regularly, throwing away any left. What is important is that hummingbirds must never be fed honey or artificial sweeteners and that any food offered must never be allowed to go stale. In hot weather sugar mixtures deteriorate rapidly and may need changing every day. Ants, wasps and other insects can also be a problem when they discover the easily obtained food for they discourage the hummingbirds and can also trigger early fermentation of the "nectar." They are, however, not easy to deter other than by using feeders with special bee guards or in the case of ants, rubbing the support wires with a sticky substance such as salad oil or moving the feeder. Fermenting substances only encourage fungal

Below right: **A Broad-billed Hummingbird (*Cynanthus latirostris*) at a garden feeder.**

Below: **Hummingbird feeders also attract wasps and other unwanted guests.**

Above left: **An Anna's Hummingbird (*Calypte anna*) attracted to a trumpet-shaped bright red hibiscus.**

Above right: **Lilies are very popular with the Broad-billed Hummingbird (*Cynanthus latirostris*).**

growths which lead to sick and dying birds so fresh food in clean containers is a must. As a rule it should be changed every two or three days.

To prepare your own hummingbird food a mixture of one part sugar to four parts drinking water should be heated and allowed to simmer for a couple of minutes to kill off any bacteria and reduce harmful chemicals. When cool, store any not used in feeders in a clean container in the refrigerator. Prepare only sufficient for a few days use at a time and thoroughly clean all containers every two or three days.

Positioning feeders around the yard or even close by the house where they can easily be observed will invariably attract hummingbirds but in general they prefer the natural nectar from flowers. The best bet to encourage hummingbirds close to your home is to adopt both methods by also planting suitable hardy herbs and shrubs that will give a succession of flowers throughout the year. Trumpet-shaped blooms, particularly red, orange, and yellow are like magnets to hummingbirds.

Trees, shrubs, and perennial plants are the least trouble when established and there are many to choose from. Even trees that are not regularly used by hummingbirds can be made use of by allowing vines such as honeysuckle, morning glory, and trumpet creeper to climb up them. Azaleas and mimosa may take time before they flower and can grow to a reasonable size and the perennial lilies, phlox, and hibiscus are not difficult to spread around the garden.

A little more effort is needed with the annual bedding plants. They not only produce a very colorful garden in their own right, but also can be extremely attractive to hummingbirds throughout the summer months. Plants to try are: begonia, foxglove, geranium, gladiolas, hollyhock, impatiens, indian paintbrush, lantana, nasturtium, nicotinia, petunia, red salvia, shrimp plant, spiderflower, sweet william, and texas olive.

As a word of warning, hummingbirds are very sensitive to pesticides and herbicides so the use of chemical sprays is to be avoided.

Hummingbirds' Symbiosis with Flowering Plants

The symbiotic relationship between hummingbirds and plants has resulted in a wide variety of adaptations between the two on which both are, as a family, mutually dependant, or at least partly so. However, there is little evidence of specific interdependence. Competition exists for nectar by bees as well as other insects, and to some extent they must all play a part in pollination.

Many hummingbirds search out large, pendant type, bell-shaped flowers that are brightly colored; usually red, orange, or yellow and often with white inner petals or corollas. Others are attracted to white flowers with red markings such as those found on some of the epiphytes. During the process of extracting nectar, plant pollination is achieved as the hummingbird transfers pollen from one flower to another. Interestingly, hummingbird-pollinated flowers are seldom scented and only infrequently attract insects. The color stimulus provided by these plants is heavily weighted towards the red end of the spectrum, the long wavelengths to which hummingbird vision is most sensitive. Hummingbirds associate these colors in flowers with food availability, in particular the energy content of the nectar.

Within many of the flowers visited by hummingbirds reside tiny mites which also feed on nectar and pollen. As the bird is feeding, mites will move onto the bill and into the nasal cavity where they are transported, unbeknown and harmless to the hummingbird, to a new host plant to commence another breeding cycle.

Below: **Hummingbirds must compete with bees and other insects at some flowers.**

Behavior

The behavior of hummingbirds is, in the main, governed by their environment and habits. Their adaptations as nectar-feeding species require that they move around according to their specialized needs and reliance on nectar-bearing food sources. Consequently, their feeding habits are solitary occupations and males and females lead completely separate lives, even becoming very aggressive to each other and also to other nectar-feeding species. They seek out those flowers which are especially energy-rich and inevitably there will be great competition around good food sources. Individuals set up territories around such flowering plants and vigorously defend them against intruders. Their aggression can be extreme to the extent of attacking anything, even humans, which they see as a potential rival for the food supply.

Leading such solitary lives leads to their polygamous breeding behavior and the very brief acts of copulation are often the only time the sexes come into contact. At the start of the breeding season the males of several hummingbird species arrive on the breeding grounds prior to the females and group together in bands, called "leks," around potentially rich food sources to vie for females as they pass by.

Hummingbirds really seem to enjoy bathing and do so several times a day often followed by vigorous shaking and long bouts of preening. Some will hover above shallow pools, suddenly dropping in and often completely submerging. Others find puddles, either on the ground or in large leaves, in which to land and then soak themselves by splashing their wings. During

Below: **Green-backed Firecrowns (*Sephanoides s.*) fighting for territory.**

Right: **A Green-backed Firecrown (*Sephanoides s.*) bathing.**

rainfall they will often sit out in the open with outstretched wings and well spread tail just catching the raindrops on their plumage. Waterfalls are another favorite place to bathe to catch falling water drops, just as are water sprinklers in parks and gardens.

Such behavior is all a necessary part of their feather care—the birds attempt to maintain the plumage in an efficient and clean condition, as they must undoubtedly become soiled with nectar and pollen during their feeding activities. After bathing, preening plays an important part in the oiling of feathers ensuring that they stay waterproof in often rainy and humid conditions.

Below left: **Female Black-chinned Hummingbird (*Archilochus alexandri*) feeding her two chicks.**

Below right: **Anna's Hummingbird (*Calypte anna*) in garden spray.**

Breeding

The very short association that the female hummingbird has with the polygynous male serves only to fertilize her eggs. She then lays two dull, white, pea-sized eggs, completing the breeding cycle completely alone.

Studies in captivity have shown that the female will only accept a male within her breeding territory for a very short period of a day or two until her eggs are fertilized, after which she will fiercely drive off any other bird. Nest-building, incubation, and rearing are all completed by the female although occasional male participation has been reported.

At the start of the breeding cycle, males adopt various methods to attract females. Their iridescent plumage is particularly conspicuous along with their enhanced song and aerial displays. The female will often perch and take up a submissive pose while the male hovers close in front of her as if to "test the water." She will either be driven away or a very short-term bond will develop until her eggs are fertilized.

Some males gather in "leks," while others remain in their feeding territories, allowing females to enter for the purpose of copulation. The behavior and posturing of the intruding female diverts the normally defensive behavior of the male to a role of sexual activity. Thereafter they both resume their solitary lifestyle.

As one would expect, the breeding cycle is geared to coincide with the peak flowering period of their major food plants. This may be for only a very short period for some high altitude areas and almost year-long for others in the lowlands.

Nest sites are quite variable between species and differ not only in the type of location but also in the height at which they are built. Often near water, many are hidden and few are very conspicuous. Cup-shaped constructions are normal, many positioned in a shaded position on the top of a twig, branch, or leaf, but others are attached to vertical surfaces or even suspended below overhanging leaves. Some species choose to construct domed or semi-domed roofs which may provide some shelter from rain or sun.

The usually tiny nests are invariably built from fine plant fibers and loosely woven with spiders' webs. They are decorated and disguised with small pieces of locally collected plant debris. Moss, lichen, leaf-litter, rootlets, pieces of bark, hairy fibers, and more spiders' webs are all used to blend in the appearance with the local environment. The cup is usually lined with softer plant fibers and plant-down with the occasional use of tiny feathers. High altitude species often have less tidy but bulkier nests, using coarser materials and hidden amongst dense, tussocky vegetation.

Above: **Hummingbirds lay two white eggs not much bigger than peas.**

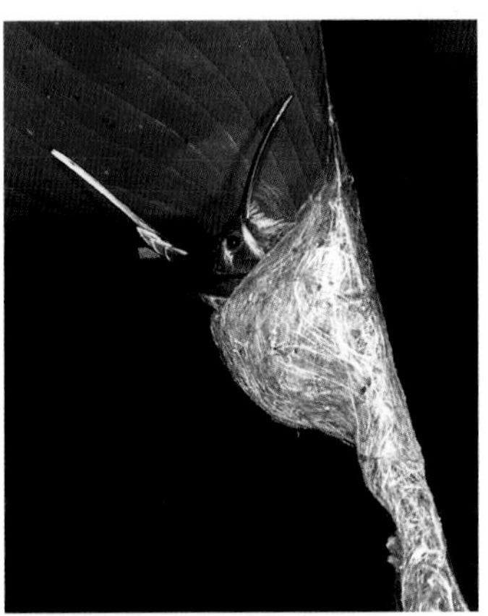

Above: **A White-bearded Hermit (*Phaethornis hispidus*) nest suspended below a large leaf.**

Above: **A Rufous Hummingbird (*Selasphorus rufus*) collecting plant down for its nest.**

Right: **A female hummingbird stimulating its chick to feed by touching its back.**

It is very unusual for more than two eggs to be laid in a clutch and when more have been found in a nest they are thought to have been deposited by another female. Incubation is around 16 to 19 days, but high altitude species can take a few days longer. The young are born denuded of almost all feathers and require a period of three to four weeks in the nest before they fledge. At birth two rows of short bristly down feathers develop along the back and the eyes are unopened. A feeding stimulus is given to the chick by the mother who touches the head or back feathers with her bill.

Only in the second week of life do the youngsters open their eyes and at this time the body feathers also really begin to show. Close to fledging, the female will hover over the nest creating a downdraught, which visibly disturbs the chick's plumage, and they start to gape for food.

Once they are out of the nest, the female continues to feed her young for another three weeks or so, but they usually remain in the close vicinity of the nest during this period, often hidden in the tree canopy. Gradually the young are persuaded by the female's persistent calls to follow her to convenient flowering plants where they will soon learn to feed for themselves.

Below left: **A female Ruby-throated Hummingbird (*Archilochus colubris*) hovering over its chick to stimulate it to gape.**

Below middle: **A fledgling Allen's Hummingbird (*Selasphorus sasin*) preparing to fly.**

Below right: **A recently fledged Andean Hillstar (*Oreotrochilus estella*) being fed.**

Left: **Frilled Coquette (*Lophornis magnificus*) display.**

Left: **Sparkling Violet-ear (*Colibri coruscans*) display.**

Left: **A Green-backed Firecrown (*Sephanoides s.*) on a lichen-decorated nest.**

Distribution, Migration, and Movements

The family of hummingbirds, the Trochilidae, are found in the neotropical regions of the New World in an area covering all of South America and its adjacent islands, northward through the Caribbean and North America as far as Nova Scotia in the east and Alaska in the west. The most northerly-breeding hummingbird is the rufous hummingbird which is found in Alaska, and the most southerly are the green-backed firecrown breeds in Tierra del Fuego. There are now thought to be 328 species of New World hummingbirds, of which Costa Rica alone has 51. The highest density of hummingbird species occurs through Colombia, Ecuador, and northern Peru, where around 150 species have been recorded.

Long distance seasonal migration of hummingbirds is limited to only a small proportion of the species; those having their breeding grounds in the USA and Canada north of the tropics, and those to the south in southern South America. However, many disperse after breeding to exploit better food resources or for more suitable climatic conditions.

In reality, the study of hummingbird movements has only just begun. Large scale bird banding of hummingbirds is both difficult and not very remunerative record-wise due not only to the size of the bird but to the chances of getting adequate returns from non-populated areas and difficult terrains.

Most of the knowledge of hummingbird movement today is concentrated around only very few species and relies on the fact that at certain times of the year birds are present or absent in a given region. It is generally surmised that birds are traveling between them. This perception goes a little further in speculating that in some species, the sexes arrive and leave at different times but there is very little known of how this correlates with the bird's age. Within the vast area of known hummingbird habitat in North America and Canada, where banding and study may be comparatively easy, much of the work is done at well-established feeding stations. It is when the birds leave these stations that the problem becomes particularly difficult. Studies in this region have shown that most North American species of hummingbird are only partial migrants. That is, there is a tendency for birds at the northern boundaries of the range to move to more favorable climates for the winter while those in acceptable conditions remain sedentary. Four North American species, Calliope, Rufous, Black-chinned, and Ruby-throated hummingbirds are exceptions in that they all migrate outside their breeding range for the winter months. It is known that the long distance journeys performed by these species, especially the Ruby-throated Hummingbird, are often non-stop

Below: **The Calliope Hummingbird (*Stellula calliope*) is the World's smallest long-distance migrant.**

Above: **The Ruby-throated Hummingbird (*Archilochus colubris*) is able to migrate 500 miles non-stop over the Gulf of Mexico. This specimen is a female.**

and even flying over the 500 or so miles of the Gulf of Mexico. It is much more likely that many take the easier but longer route around the gulf. Whichever way it is an incredible feat especially for the Calliope Hummingbird, the world's smallest long distance migrant.

As with other species of long distance migratory bird, hummingbirds need to put on body fat if they are to undertake long journeys without feeding. Increases in body weight prior to venturing out on long migrations can be as much as 60 per cent for the Broad-tailed Hummingbird, 50 per cent for Anna's Hummingbird, and a remarkable 100 per cent for the Ruby-throated Hummingbird.

Even within the tropics a certain amount of migrational movement takes place. Banding records within Brazil show seasonal long distance movements for some species.

Except when the journeys are over water, the pattern of movements is far from simple. Even within the same species different types of movement can be observed. Post-breeding dispersal is frequently accompanied by altitudinal movements of juvenile birds into food-rich alpine grasslands, but for some species a number of adults also join them. The remaining adults may move to lower altitudes and many will migrate out of the area altogether. This pattern of movement is adopted by Anna's Hummingbird which breeds in the Californian lowlands with many birds dispersing eastward as far as the Sierras after breeding and finally moving on again into New Mexico for the winter.

Within most of the hummingbird species inhabiting the Andes, altitudinal movements are probably much more common. Weather conditions and availability of food sources are conditions which the birds need to exploit so altitudinal migration is essential for survival.

Scientific Study of Hummingbirds

It is only by the close study and observation of hummingbirds that their true status can be determined. Being such small and rather difficult to observe birds raises many problems for the scientists trying to gain knowledge of them. The study of movement and migration requires that birds are marked individually so that they may be recognized later in their life wherever they may be found, so at some time they must be caught. The process of trapping the birds and applying small, very lightweight individually marked rings or bands is the normal procedure. The whole process from making the tiny ring to attaching it to the short thin leg of a hummingbird is a daunting task. It demands great care and patience and enormous skill; the bird must not be harmed or unduly disturbed from its previous activities. Any serious diversion from its normal behavior would be counter-productive.

The very small size of the band limits the amount of information it can carry and this is confined to a unique coded number, which also denotes its place of ringing. The band itself must have smooth edges to prevent abrasions on the leg and when it is closed around the leg there must be no gaps or edges which may allow it to become entangled with anything the bird perches on.

Handling the tiny living body of a hummingbird is a task that requires very special technique and care, and only a very small and dedicated band of banders are licensed to carry out the work. They are usually based at recognized observatories and field stations often in areas where, for one reason or another, hummingbirds are known to frequent.

Below: **The outside diameter of this hummingbird ring is only $\frac{5}{64}$" (2mm), so small that you could fit at least 65 on top of a penny.**

Such an observatory is the Southeastern Arizona Bird Observatory (SABO) at Bisbee in Arizona run by Director/Naturalist, Sheri Williamson. Here hummingbirds are caught in mist nets; very soft and fine nets suspended on taught strings attached between two rigid poles. The nets are so fine that when viewed straight-on they are almost invisible. When placed against the background of a bush and in the flight path of a bird, the bird cannot see it and is therefore caught. It falls harmlessly in a pocket of the net and lies there for the few moments taken for the bander to reach it. Once removed from the net, birds are identified and banded, and biometric

Left: **Only well-experienced, licenced bird banders are allowed to use mist nets for catching hummingbirds. Here a mist net is set up near an artificial feeder and a bird is being extracted from the net.**

data including weighing, measuring, and plumage details are recorded. They are then allowed a small feed from an artificial feeder while still in the hand before being released back to the wild.

The amassed data can be analyzed to study many different aspects of hummingbird biology as well as population levels and birds re-trapped in other places can contribute to our knowledge of lifespan, migration, and movement.

Below left: **Using a ruler to measure the folded wing-length of a Calliope Hummingbird (*Stellula calliope*).**

Below right: **Here a Black-chinned Hummingbird (*Archilochus alexandri*) is being weighed with a spring balance.**

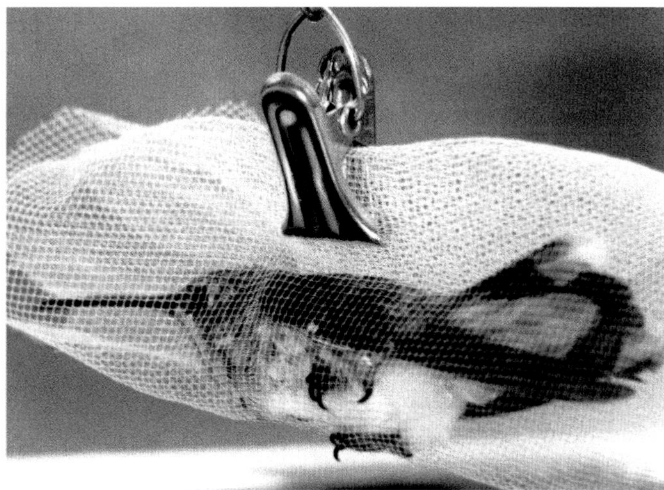

A Gallery of Hummingbirds

White-tipped Sicklebill

Eutoxeres aquila

4¾–5½" (12–14cm)

This is a fairly common hummingbird within its range and is often known by several other common names, in particular Common, White, Brown-tailed, or Bronze Sicklebill. There are three races—the nominate and more easterly *E. a. aquila* found in the eastern Andes from northern Peru to Colombia. *E. a. heterura* ranges through the western Andes from Ecuador into southwest Colombia, while *E. a. salvini* is spread through western Colombia and up through Panama into Costa Rica. It is sedentary through most of its range being found more in foothill areas with water present; in particular in or close by humid forest and forest edges. Heliconia is a favorite feeding plant, as are other plants suited to its sickle-shaped bill. It also takes spiders and many insects. This is one of the few hummingbirds that prefer to perch when feeding.

The markedly decurved bill of this hummingbird is a great aid to identification. Apart from the Buff-tailed Sicklebill (*Eutoxeres condamini*) it has the most strongly accentuated decurved bill of all hummingbirds. Fortunately the two are easily separated by the more buffish plumage and buff tail coloring as they overlap in range in south Colombia and Peru. The White-tailed Sicklebill has darkish-green upperparts including the crown and nape. The rounded bronzy-green tail has white tips, more obvious in the nominate race. Underparts are white streaked black with undertail coverts edged pale reddish-brown. The bill is blackish and feet brown. Females are very similar to males although having slightly shorter wings.

Breeding takes place from January in the north of the range through to September in the south. A suspended woven cup-shaped nest is constructed at the tip of a drooping leaf with a mass of plant fibers and tiny rootlets bound together and onto its support by means of spiders' webs. The female incubates her two eggs for two and a half weeks and the chicks fledge some three and a half weeks later.

Hairy Hermit

Glaucis hirsuta

4¾" (12cm)

The other common name for this species is the Rufous-breasted Hermit and two races are recognized. The northerly race *G. h. insularum* is isolated on the islands of Trinidad, Tobago, and Grenada. The nominate race *G. h. hirsuta* is very much more widespread, covering nearly all of Brazil apart from the far south and far northeast; then almost all of the remainder of northern South America east of the Andes including the Guianas, Venezuela, Colombia, Panama, Peru, and Bolivia. This species is common over much of its range particularly in the Amazonas. It is thought to be sedentary, keeping to the lowlands where it can be found in a great diversity of habitats. However, it is never far from trees even when present in areas of grassland. Not only does it enjoy dense woodland and thickets, it also frequents clearings and forest edges and is often found in marshland and riverine habitats. It is a nectar feeder and seeks out flowers of trees, shrubs, and vines often being seen at heliconia. Small insects and spiders are also gleaned from the foliage.

The male's upperparts are bronze-green and the underparts reddish brown, becoming brown at the chin and flanks. The underbelly is off-white. The roundish tail has white-tipped feathers, the central two being green and the outers reddish brown at the base with a broad black sub-terminal band. His slightly decurved bill is black above and buffish-orange below. The female, although similar, is much paler over the throat and upper-breast and her bill is more decurved.

The northerly race has a breeding season spread over the first six months of the year whereas for the nominate race it is more dependant on its location. A cup-shaped nest is constructed with pieces of plant fiber, leaf, and a few spiders' webs and suspended from the underside of a drooping leaf with similar materials. The whole of the outside is decorated with pieces of lichen, bark, and tiny twigs. Normally two eggs are incubated by the female for nearly three weeks. The chicks fledge around three to four weeks later.

Green Hermit

Phaethornis guy

5" (1.3cm)

Known also as Guy's Hermit or the White-tailed Hermit, there are four races, the nominate, *P. g. guy,* being concentrated in Trinidad and an area of northeast Venezuela. The western race, *P. g. coruscans* is isolated in an area from northwest Colombia and through Costa Rica. *P. g. emiliae* is spread through the less mountainous regions and river valleys of northwest Colombia and *P. g. apicalis* inhabits the Andes eastern mountain slopes from Southern Peru up into northwest Venezuela. Although they may frequently be seen close to forest edges and in clearings, they seem to prefer the seclusion of more dense undergrowth especially associated with humid forest. They take nectar from a wide variety of flowers of shrubs, trees, and other plants, and also glean for insects and spiders.

Birds of the nominate race are the largest and have mildly iridescent all-green upperparts and dullish bronze-green underparts tinged gray. A blackish green patch extends from the lore (the space between the bill and the eye) and below the eye to the ear coverts. A buffish orange post-ocular stripe is sometimes evident. The upper-tail coverts have an emerald-green hue leading into the base of the tail feathers which have a broad black band across the tips. The central tail feathers of the predominantly rounded tail are slightly extended at the tips. The long, slightly decurved bill is black above and the lower mandible orange-brown toward the base. There is also an orange-brown gular stripe. Females usually have shorter bills and wings and the narrow central tail feather extensions are considerably longer and almost white at the tips. The outer tail feathers also have white tips. They have more obvious gular and post ocular orange-buff stripes. Of all the races, *P. g. coruscans* has the most brilliant plumage even showing some iridescence on the underparts.

Breeding sites are usually close to water. A long, pendulous, conical construction is suspended from the tip of a long drooping leaf. Plant fibers along with spiders' webs and pieces of lichen are combined in the loose cup-shape and suspension. Although the males remain in the vicinity of the nest, it is the female which does the incubation. The two eggs hatch after two and a half weeks, the chicks taking a further three and a half weeks to fledge.

White-bearded Hermit

Phaethornis hispidus

5" (13cm)

Also referred to as d'Osery's Hermit, this bird prefers the humid lowland forests east of the Andes covering a large area of northern South America including Venezuela, Colombia, Ecuador, Peru, Bolivia and the Western Amazonas of Brazil. It occurs particularly in damp situations by rivers and in swamp forests as well as bamboo stands. It takes nectar from flowering trees, shrubs, and epiphytes and is especially attracted by heliconia. Small insects and flies are also taken by gleaning.

It is of typical hermit appearance having bronze-green upperparts with a grayish tinge over the crown and gray edges to the upper-tail coverts. The feathers of the predominantly rounded tail are dark bronze-green tipped white with the central two feathers extended into narrow white tips. Underparts are gray with a distinct off-white gular stripe leading up to the chin. The dark ear coverts are bordered by a white malar stripe and another white stripe to the rear. The bill is blackish and decurved, more accentuated in the female.

The breeding season is very dependent on the location; taking place almost throughout the year. A suspended nest of plant fibers is bound together and attached to an overhanging leaf with spiders' webs. The clutch of two eggs is incubated for about two and a half weeks, the young fledging around three weeks later.

Reddish Hermit

Phaethornis ruber

3½" (9cm)

This small hermit also takes the names of Pygmy Hermit and Red-vented Hermit, there being four races distributed in the northern half of South America east of the Andes. The nominate race *P. r. ruber* covers a band from French Guiana and Surinam through the Amazonas of Brazil and into northern Bolivia and southeastern Peru. *P. r. longipennis* is from southern Peru, *P. r. nigricinctus* is from northern Peru and north-eastwards through eastern Colombia and just into southern Venezuela and *P. r. episcopus* is spread through central and eastern Venezuela eastwards to French Guiana and south into northern Brazil. It is another fairly common lowland species keeping in or near to forests. Sub-montane forest, deciduous forest as well as secondary growth and thickets are all suitable habitats where they search for flowering plants. Nectar is taken both by hover-feeding as well as by piercing the flower base. Numerous insects are also gleaned from foliage.

The male has iridescent bronzy-green forehead, crown, nape, mantle, and wing coverts. The underparts and rump are reddish brown-cinnamon and there is a dark band, sometimes almost black, across the breast. His almost black ear coverts are bordered at the rear by a whitish stripe and at the front by a thin white malar stripe. Rufous upper-tail coverts lead into rounded tail feathers which are reddish-brown at the base becoming darker towards a black sub-terminal band and then narrowly tipped pale rufous. His slightly decurved bill is mainly black but pale rufous at the base of the lower mandible. The female is paler on the underparts with a less obvious dark patch in the center of the breast and her slightly longer tail feathers have broader rufous tips.

Breeding takes place from May to October, the season varying considerably with location. The nest, a suspended cone-shape with the cup at the base is usually attached to the underside of a long pendulous leaf. Spiders' webs are used to attach the nest to the leaf and to bind together the plant fibers, lichen, moss, and leaf pieces. The female incubates her two eggs for just over two weeks and the young fledge some two and a half to three weeks later.

Green-fronted Lancebill

Doryfera ludovicae

5" (13cm)

This species inhabits the humid forests and wet cloudforests from Costa Rica and Panama as well as the Andes from western Venezuela in the north through Colombia, Ecuador, and Peru down into northwest Bolivia. The race *D. l. veraguensis* is found in an area from the northern central part of Costa Rica eastwards to western Panama, the nominate race being found elsewhere in the range. During the breeding season, the Green-fronted Lancebill prefers to remain within forest seeking out nectar from the long tubular flowers of epiphytes to which it is so well adapted. However, after breeding it begins to explore outside the forest canopy, along the edges and in clearings wherever the long tubular flowers are present. Not only does it take nectar from the flowers by hovering beneath them; it will also glean insects and spiders from foliage in a similar manner. Sometimes it even hawks for flying insects.

This species has a comparatively long and slightly upturned black bill and the forehead is brilliant iridescent green. Crown, nape, and sides of the head are iridescent copper-brown becoming coppery-green on the back down to the blue-gray rump. The dark-gray to black rounded tail has pale grayish tips and the underparts are dull bronze-green. Females usually have a smaller iridescent forehead patch which is sometimes missing altogether.

The breeding season, starting in late July, extends through to January. The nest, a substantial cup-shape of mosses, plant fibers, and pieces of treefern bound together with spiders' webs is attached to a suspended rootlet or twig, most often in a shaded position. Two eggs are typically incubated for about two and a half weeks with the young fledging almost a month later.

Violet Sabrewing

Campylopterus hemileucurus

5¾" (15cm)

Another common name for this brilliantly colored hummingbird is de Lattre's Sabrewing. The nominate and more northerly of the two races, *C. h. hemileucurus*, is found in an area of the central highlands stretching from southern Chiapas in Mexico through Guatemala, Honduras, and Nicaragua to the border with Costa Rica although other isolated populations exist in northern Guatemala and southern Mexico. *C. h. mellitus* ranges from western Costa Rica to western Panama. Throughout its range, this largish hummingbird has adapted well to the changes brought about by man and now occurs close to human habitation in yards and gardens, plantations, and disturbed areas of agriculture. Its main habitat however lies on the mountain slopes and foothills where they are close to the edges of humid forest and frequently in association with riverine habitat by streams. Within forest it keeps below the canopy, seeking out flowers of shrubs and vines in search of nectar. It also takes numerous insects and spiders by foraging through undergrowth and gleaning from foliage and occasionally snatching flies from the air.

The male has brilliant violet-blue breast, throat, nape, and upper-back with the lower-back becoming a dark green. The forehead also has a green tinge. The mainly dark blue-black tail is squarish and has broad white tips on the outer three feathers; very visible in flight. The wings are brownish black with obviously more substantial shafts to the first two primary feathers creating the shape of a saber. There is a white spot at the rear of the eye and the black bill is decurved. The female lacks the violet coloring and has greenish upperparts becoming bronze-green on the crown. Her breast is gray leading up to a violet throat. She also has a more decurved bill than the male. The male of *C. h. mellitus* is very much more violet than the violet-blue of the nominate race.

Breeding occurs during the wet season when a substantial nest of moss is constructed on a thin horizontal branch overhanging water. The moss is neatly interwoven with plant fibers and bound together with spiders' webs. No further reliable breeding information is available.

White-necked Jacobin

Florisuga mellivora

4¾" (12cm)

Other common names for this medium sized hummingbird are Collared Hummingbird and the Jacobin. There are two races; the more confined and slightly larger race *F. m. flabellifera* being found only on Tobago. The nominate race, *F. m. mellivora* however has a very broad range from southern Mexico eastward through to Panama and Colombia and then spread over most of the Amazonas southward to Matto Grosso and eastward to Goyaz and Maranhao, taking in the Guianas and Trinidad. More often found in the lowlands, it sometimes ventures into the foothills but seldom above 5,000ft (1,500m). It prefers high trees both in plantations or humid forest but is frequently found in open woodland and secondary forest. Although it regularly hawks for insects and flies, it feeds mainly on nectar from flowering trees and shrubs and can frequently be seen at flowering epiphytes and heliconia.

The male has an outstanding dark-blue head, neck, and chest. Between the nape and upper-back is a distinct white collar. The rest of the upperparts are brilliant dark green stretching down over the rump to extended upper-tail coverts. The belly is white, as is the squarish tail, which has a narrow black terminal band. The very slightly decurved bill is black. The typical female plumage has all green upperparts and a whitish belly. The breast and throat feathers often appear mainly green with fine whitish edges forming a regular pattern but this can be very variable. The tail feathers, including the extended upper-tail coverts are a dark green-blue with fine white tips.

The breeding season is very variable throughout the range but occurs mainly at the end of the dry season and into the wet. Nest sites are frequently chosen where there is protection from above such as a large leaf but frequently only a few feet above the ground. Very fine plant fibers are bound together with spiders' webs into a small bowl shape nest. No other breeding data is available.

Green Violet-ear

Colibri thalassinus

4½" (11½cm)

This species includes races which have, in the past, been considered as individual species in their own right. *C. t. cyanotus* was previously called the Mountain Violet-ear and *C. t. thalassinus*, now the nominate race, was called the Mexican Violet-ear. The nominate and more northerly race, *C. t. thalassinus*, occasionally found in the far southeastern United States ranges mainly from central Mexico southward and well into northern Nicaragua. From there *C. t. cabanidis* is found, its range extending further south through Costa Rica and into the hills of western Panama. The range of *C. t. cyanotus* covers the mountainous regions of Ecuador, Colombia, and Venezuela. The most southerly race, *C. t. crissalis* keeps to the Andes mountains through Peru and Bolivia and down into northern Argentina. Although primarily a mountain species, they are found at lower altitudes, particularly when dispersing after the breeding season. Preferring a more open habitat with a scattering of trees and shrubs, they can often be found close to farm and pastureland, sometimes venturing into plantations, yards, and gardens with a profusion of flowering shrubs. Besides feeding from nectar they frequently take spiders and small insects by either gleaning them from hedgerows or hawking.

The plumage of the nominate race is predominantly iridescent bluish green with blackish wings and a glittering dark blue-green patch on the upper breast. At the lower breast and vent the plumage becomes dull gray. Iridescent blue-green feathers of the throat, often extending down into the breast, have blackish spots in their centers. The ear-coverts, which extend down to the neck, are a dark violet which glistens silver-blue in certain lights. The bluish green coloring of the back continues down into the central feathers of the rather square tail; the outer tail feathers appearing more turquoise-blue. There is a dark sub-terminal band across all of the tail. The slightly curved bill and the feet are black. Females may appear a little less bright in plumage and are very slightly smaller in size. The plumage of other races, although very similar, are lacking in the dark blue-green patch on the upper-breast.

The breeding season can be from July through to March depending on local conditions but usually coinciding with the end of the wet season. The substantial cup-shaped nest, often low down, is frequently positioned precariously on a thin twig or root. Fine grasses, moss, plant down, and bits of tree-fern are all bound together with spiders' webs and lined with fine plant fibers before being decorated externally with lichen and fragments of leaf and bark. Two eggs are incubated for around two and a half weeks and the young can take as long as four weeks to fledge.

Sparkling Violet-ear

Colibri coruscans

5–5½" (13–14cm)

Also known by the common names of Chequered, Gould's, or Colombian Violet-ear, the species consists of only two races. The nominate race *C. c. coruscans* ranges from the northwest tip of Venezuela through western Columbia, Ecuador, and Peru into western Bolivia and the northwest of Argentina. The subspecies *C. c. germanus* is found in northern South America, across southern Venezuela eastward to Guiana, taking in the northern fringes of Brazil.

This is a species, which prefers a habitat of open woodland, and forest edges and frequently occurs close to habitation in plantations and yards. It is also often found in ornamental gardens and parks in large cities. Birds occurring at low elevations tend to be sedentary with only small dispersal movements after breeding. At higher elevations it inhabits areas prolific in pàramo plants often above 5,500ft (1,700m) and even up to 14,000ft (4,400m) above sea level. These birds migrate to lower elevations during the dry season when the food plants become scarce.

It has adapted to a very wide range of food plants and feeds from ground level to the treetops. Its basic diet is flower nectar supplemented with insects, gleaned from plants or hawked in the air.

Male birds have bluish green upperparts with a metallic sheen. The underparts are the same color but there is a bluish patch in the center of the belly and also under the chin. The dark blue ear coverts consist of extended feathers, which can be raised in display. In favorable lighting conditions, the blue areas can show an intense purple iridescence. The dark tail is a metallic blue-green with a suggestion of a darker blue sub-terminal band. Females have very similar coloration and also a small white spot just behind the eye. The sub-species *C. c. germanus* can be distinguished by its bluer underparts and tail and the area at the front of the crown.

Breeding occurs from early July through to October. The nest, often on top of a horizontal branch or in a cavity amongst rocks is cup-shaped, consisting of fine plant fibers decorated externally with pieces of lichen and small twigs, although some birds create a suspended structure from the end of a branch. The female incubates a clutch of two eggs for up to 18 days. The young fledge after three weeks in the nest.

Black-throated Mango

Anthracothorax nigricollis

4½–4¾" (11–12cm)

The range of this species is vast, covering the greater part of northern South America from western Panama to the Guianas, including Trinidad and Tobago in the north, to south Brazil, taking in much of Peru, Bolivia, Paraguay, and the north of Argentina. This is one of the more common species of hummingbird in the tropical areas of its range especially at low elevations where it can even be seen within cities. It likes a more open habitat with a few trees and shrubs—often very close to human habitation. Gardens, yards, and parkland are visited frequently as well as agricultural land, but it can also be found on the lower cultivated hillsides. It takes nectar from tall flowering trees and shrubs as well as hawking for insects.

The upperparts of both male and female are bright bronze-green. The male has a dense black strip from the chin to the breast, which is edged with iridescent blue-green particularly at the neck, and green at the flanks. The central tail feathers are bronze-green edged black and the outers reddish-brown with a purple sheen and finely edged blue toward the tips. His black bill is lightly decurved. The female is very similar to the male but lacks the blue-green border to the black breast stripe. She has a white border instead running from the base of the bill right down the flanks. Her tail is also similar to that of the male but has a dark, almost black, sub-terminal band and whitish tips.

Breeding takes place during the first six months of the year and a nest site is chosen high in trees on top of an exposed branch. The cup-shaped nest consisting of fine plant fibers and a few spiders' webs is decorated externally with pieces of lichen. The female incubates her two eggs for two and a half weeks and the young fledge about three and a half weeks later. It is known that this species often attempts two broods in a season.

Green Mango

Anthracothorax viridis

4½–5½" (11–14cm)

Found only in Puerto Rico and also known as the Puerto Rican Mango, this small hummingbird is more likely to be seen in forests and plantations of the central and western mountains. It seldom appears around the more densely populated human habitation around the coast. Feeding on nectar, it searches out flowers from a wide variety of trees, shrubs, and vines. It also gleans over foliage for insects and spiders and hawks for flying insects from the treetops.

The plumage of both sexes is very similar; appearing a metallic green except for the rounded tail, which is a shining blackish blue becoming blacker towards the tip. The underparts often have a blue tinge. The sexes can only be separated in the adult plumage when the females have a small white spot behind the eye that is always missing in the male.

During the long breeding season, which starts as early as October and carries on through to May, only a single brood is attempted. The tiny cup-shaped nest, built of plant fibers and down and disguised on the outside with pieces of lichen is usually located high in trees attached to an upright stem. The clutch of two eggs takes a little over two weeks to incubate, the young fledging some three to four weeks later.

Jamaican Mango

Anthracothorax mango

4¾" (12cm)

This dark colored little mango is found only in Jamaica where it is also known as the Black Mango. It is a resident and fairly common species especially along the north coast of the island. Its main habitat lies in more open areas of the lowlands as well as plantation and forest boundaries. Agricultural land, parkland, yards, and gardens particularly in the vicinity of flowering trees are also frequently occupied. Nectar from a wide variety of flowering, trees, shrubs, herbs, and succulents make up a large proportion of the diet, although it is supplemented with numerous aerial insects which are caught in flight.

Both male and female are very similar in plumage having dark bronze-green upperparts with a greenish tinge over the crown. The central tail feathers are a dull, dark bronze and all the outer feathers a dark violet with a blue sheen terminating in a dark blue band. The underparts are black, almost velvet in appearance and the ear coverts and sides of the head are iridescent purple, red, and blue. The slightly curved bill is all black. Females can sometimes be separated by having a greenish tinge to the otherwise black flanks and they have small white tips to the outer tail feathers.

Breeding can take place at any time throughout the year but is more prevalent during the first few months. The tiny, cup-shaped nest, usually situated on top of a branch fairly high in a tree, is constructed from fine soft plant fibers bound up with spiders' webs. A clutch of two eggs is incubated by the female for two and a half to three weeks.

Ruby Topaz Hummingbird

Chrysolampis mosquitus

3¼–3½" (8–9cm)

Also known as just the Ruby Topaz, this is one of the better known of the hummingbirds. It has brilliant coloration and was at one time exported throughout the world from Brazil for the pet trade. It also has a quite widespread distribution over the northern part of South America extending down in the east through most of northern and central Brazil and into eastern Bolivia. It also occurs throughout the islands fringing the north coast from Trinidad and Tobago in the east to Aruba in the west. Breeding birds prefer the lowland regions with open grassland and scattered trees as well as cultivated land and gardens.

They seek out nectar bearing flowers from a wide variety of plants, shrubs, trees, and cacti both wild and cultivated as well as hawking for insects and gleaning along hedgerows for small spiders.

The brilliance of color reflected by this bird's iridescent plumage is particularly noticeable. Males have a ruby-red crown and nape sometimes tinged with orange and brightly iridescent warm yellow upper breast. In some birds the upper breast is greenish. The back, lower breast, and underparts are dark brown with an olive sheen and the tail is a dark chestnut with a black tip. Females lack the bright iridescent red and yellow of the head and breast and have mainly olive-green upper parts and dirty white underparts. Birds from Trinidad and Tobago occasionally have a small, iridescent green, elongated throat patch. The central tail feathers are an olive-green color, whereas the remainder are chestnut with a dark sub-terminal band and white tips.

The Caribbean Island and more northerly birds choose to breed from December to June whereas those from the south in Brazil start some two months earlier finishing in January. Their very ornate and tiny cup-shaped nest is a mass of very fine plant fibers bound up with spider's webs and covered externally with pieces of moss, lichen, and small bark flakes. It is secured in the fork of a tree or shrub usually two or three meters above ground and very occasionally much higher. Normally two eggs are laid, being incubated for a little over two weeks, and the young fledging in about three weeks.

Tufted Coquette

Lophornis ornatus

2¾" (7cm)

This small hummingbird is also known as the Splendid Coquette being found not only on Trinidad but also over a large area covering the Guianas and taking in eastern Venezuela and part of northern Brazil north of the Amazon. It is a sedentary species inhabiting a wide variety of habitats but keeping more into the open such as savannas, thickets, forest edges, and even into plantations and agricultural land close to human habitation. It seems to prefer more lowland areas but is also recorded in mountainous regions. Relying mainly on nectar from a wide variety of flowers it also catches insects and spiders by gleaning, and sometimes hawks for flies.

Although occurring in a completely separate region, the male Tufted Coquette can be confused with several of the other coquettes; its main difference being in the long pale rufous fan of feathers emanating from behind the cheek. Each of these feathers terminates in a green iridescent spot. Females differ in having almost all-rufous underparts. Like the Frilled Coquette (*Lophornis magnificus*), the male has a long dark rufous crest rising from an iridescent green forehead. The upperparts are a bright iridescent green set off by a white band across the top of the bronze-tinged rump. The central feathers of the rather straight tail are also bronze-green, the outer feathers being rufous. The gorget is a shining emerald-green contrasting with lighter green underparts. His short straight bill is red tipped black. The female lacks the crest and elongated cheek feathers, having all green upperparts except for a buffish white rump band and bronze rump. Her tail feathers are tipped pale rufous and her bill is reddish brown tipped black.

Breeding occurs mainly in the dry season when a nest is built low down on a branch. It is constructed from a mixture of plant fibers often intermixed with pieces of moss and spiders' web. Two eggs are incubated by the female for two weeks, the young taking up to three weeks to fledge.

Frilled Coquette

Lophornis magnificus

3" (7½cm)

The range of this species covers an area bounded by the east coast of Brazil from Santa Catarina in the south almost to San Salvador in the north, and then westward in an arc taking in Goiás and part of Mato Grosso. Their preferred habitat is the edge of humid forest but they will readily accept man-made habitats such as plantations and areas of secondary growth. They also take readily to parks, yards, and gardens well stocked with flowering plants. Nectar from smaller flowering plants seems to be the most attractive to this species although they also consume small insects and spiders.

The male has bronze-green upperparts and both forehead and throat are iridescent emerald green. The green crown is covered by a distinct long russet crest which extends backward way over the neck. Feathers extending from the throat and behind the chin form a fan shape. Each feather, being white and terminating in a narrow iridescent green band, can give the appearance of a series of concentric crescents. There is a distinct white band across the top of the rump, the rather square tail and upper-tail coverts are bronze-colored, and the underparts are gray-green. The relatively short and straight bill is red, tipped black. Females have neither the crest nor ear tufts and apart from dirty gray-green underparts the rest of the body plumage is similar but duller. Her forehead and crown are tinged red and the throat is dirty white with a fine pattern of rufous and dark brown crescents. The tail feathers are also slightly different being more rufous at the tail coverts changing to dark bronze toward the end but tipped with pale rufous spots.

Breeding can take place from August to mid-March when a cup-shaped nest is constructed from moss, plant fibers, and down, and decorated externally with small pieces of lichen. The female incubates her two eggs for a little under two weeks and it is about three weeks before the young fledge.

Black-crested Coquette

Lophornis helenae

2" (7cm)

Also known as Princess Helena's Coquette, this small hummingbird prefers a somewhat open lowland and foothill habitat particularly at forest edges. Its main range forms a band from Vera Cruz in southern Mexico eastward through northern Oaxaca, northern Chiapas, northern Guatemala, then along the northern coast of Honduras and Nicaragua right through to eastern Costa Rica. Another population is spread through the Pacific lowlands of Guatemala. It feeds mainly from nectar from flowering trees and shrubs as well as gleaning insects and spiders from foliage and branches.

The male of this species has an iridescent green crown which is extended backward in long, thin, hair-like black feathers. The upperparts are bronze-green from the back of the head down to the central tail feathers apart from a pale, buff orange band that carries right across the top of the slightly blackish green rump. The tail is forked, the orange-buff outer feathers being edged blackish green. The gorget is a bright iridescent green bordered on the upper breast by a dark band. The remainder of the underparts are white with iridescent bronze-colored spots. The three extended feathers at the lower rear edge of the gorget are dark on the outer web and buff on the inner. He has a short red bill, tipped black. The female has no crest, the crown being bronze-green, neither does she have the green gorget and extended cheek feathers. Instead she has white underparts covered in small iridescent bronze spots apart from a bronze band across the upper-breast. Her undertail coverts are russet-cinnamon and outer-tail feathers have a broad green-black sub-terminal band.

It is thought this species nests well above the ground and consequently no reliable breeding information is available.

Wire-crested Thorntail

Discosura popelairii

male: 4½" (11½cm)

female: 3" (7½cm)

Also known as Popelair's Coquette, this seemingly rare species is usually found in the humid forests of the foothills east of the Andes in an arc ranging from central Colombia in the north through eastern Ecuador and southward into central Peru. It is one of those birds of which little is known because of its apparently shy habits and its tendency to remain high in the tree canopy. It does not adapt well to man-made habitats and is therefore likely to suffer from destruction of natural forest bordering on its current range. It feeds on nectar from flowering trees in particular the inga and it also gleans for insects and spiders.

Its name aptly describes the outstanding feature of the male of this delightful little hummingbird—a long crest of thin, almost hair-like, plumes balanced at the other end of its body by a tail of equally narrow but longer feathers. These are shown off to their best in display when the crest is pushed forward along with the tail to confront the female. The crown, crest, and throat of the male are an iridescent green as are the upper mantle, whereas the nape and back are tinged copper-green. Across the top of the rump is a distinct white band, below which the rump becomes almost black blue in the center with small areas of green at the sides. The blackish blue tail feathers all show white shafts. The breast is very dark brown, becoming white at the vent. The wings are black, as is the short straight bill. The female lacks the crest plumes and the long tail but otherwise has similarly colored upperparts. She has a dark throat patch, finely speckled white, and a distinct white malar stripe. Her slightly forked tail has white tipped feathers.

Very little is known of its breeding habits except that this occurs around April and its chosen nest sites are upon very high branches.

Red-billed Streamertail

Trochilus polytmus

Male: 11¾" (30cm)

Female: 4¼" (10½cm)

Other names for this spectacular bird are Western Streamertail or Jamaican Doctor Bird. It is quite a common species throughout Jamaica except in the very east of the island where it is replaced by the Black-billed Streamertail (*Trochilus scitulus*). It readily occupies habitats close to human habitation being found in yards, gardens, and parkland and throughout cultivated areas. It seems to be more numerous at around the 3,000ft (1,000m) altitude where it forages around clearings and forest edges, but can be found at higher altitudes when birds disperse after breeding. Not only does it take nectar from a very wide variety of flowering plants, it also takes many insects by gleaning through foliage or even from spiders' webs. It frequently hawks for aerial insects and has a habit of visiting and licking sap from holes in trees made by woodpeckers as well as extracting nectar from flowers previously pierced at their base by Bananaquits (*Coereba flaveola*).

Apart from the male's black head and the feathers of the extended crown, nape, and ear-coverts, his main body plumage is a bright iridescent emerald-green. The deeply forked tail is black with the second outer feathers extended to form long streamers which are typically crossed when perched. The edges of these two feathers are corrugated on the inner webs giving a crinkled appearance. His almost straight bill is pinkish-red and tipped black. The female lacks the black plumage of the male and has all green upperparts. Her white underparts become spotted with green at the flanks, while her short forked tail has all green feathers at the center—the dark-blue outers being clearly tipped white.

Breeding seems to take place throughout the year and as many as three broods are frequently attempted. Usually a low nest site is chosen, upon a thin branch or plant frond. The cup-shaped nest, mainly of fine plant fibers is interwoven with spiders' webs and decorated with small pieces of lichen. The female incubates her two eggs for almost three weeks and it takes about another three weeks before the young fledge.

Blue-chinned Sapphire

Chlorostilbon notatus

3–3½" (8–9cm)

Another common name for this species is Audebert's Hummingbird. There are three subspecies known at present although it has in the past been speculated that there are more. However, it is now thought that others could be hybrids with other hummingbird species. The range covered is northern South America, *C. n. notatus*, occurring along a broad coastal belt from eastern Colombia through Venezuela and the Guianas right round to the eastern tip of Brazil, also taking in Trinidad and Tobago. *C. n. puruensis* covers an area to the north of the Amazon from the northeast tip of Peru through western Colombia and southern Venezuela to the river Trombetas. The much smaller area covered by *C. n. obsoletus* is in northeast Peru. All are thought to be sedentary with only small movements due to dispersal after breeding.

It is a nectar feeder, depending very much on low flowering plants and bushes, but it also takes numerous insects and spiders, which it gleans from hedgerows and hawks in the air. It appears quite a common species, probably because of its feeding habits. It is regularly seen in town parks and gardens as well as domestic yards and around cultivated land. Woodland edges and savanna are other favorite haunts.

Males have upperparts that are a metallic bronze-green and underparts of green, slightly tinted with blue at the throat and yellow on the breast. The forked tail is gray-blue. The shortish, straight red bill has a black tip. Females are very similar but show white underparts with iridescent green spots, particularly on the throat and breast.

Its breeding season occurs from late July to November. The nest site is often very close to the ground, usually about three feet (one meter), on top of a slender branch or root. The tiny cup-shaped nest consists of fine plant fibers bound together with spiders' webs and decorated with pieces of leaf, lichen, small twigs, and bark. The lining is usually the downy fibers from seeding plants. The female incubates two eggs for just over two weeks and the young fledge after another three.

Glittering-bellied Emerald

Chlorostilbon aureoventris

3–4⅛" (9½–10½cm)

Also known as Pucheran's Emerald, there are four races, all sedentary. The race *C. a. pucherani* is found only in the east of Brazil and is slightly smaller than the nominate race *C. a. aureoventris,* which exists through Paraguay, Bolivia, and the area of Brazil bordering those two countries. *C.a. igneus* lives in northwest Argentina and *C. a. berlepschi* ranges through southern Brazil and Uraguay to the northeastern part of Argentina. Its range covers a broad spectrum of habitats from the tropical and sub-tropical forest margins of the Andean foothills in Bolivia to semi-desert, dry savanna, and grassland regions. It can often be found in city parkland and yards where it forages through the tree-tops for nectar from flowers and fruit. Occasionally it can be seen hawking amongst swarms of small insects.

The nominate race illustrated has dark green upperparts with a golden tinge blending into a paler green band of upper-tail coverts that merge into a dark gray-blue, slightly forked, tail. The breast and belly are bright iridescent bronze-green, becoming blue toward the throat. Both the forehead and crown are bronze-green. The bill is red, tipped with black. Females' upperparts and head are slightly yellower than males and they also have a grayish white streak trailing back behind the eye. Her underparts lack the green, being white turning to a whitish-buff at the breast and lower belly.

The main breeding season is from August to mid-November when a tiny cup-shaped nest is constructed on a small branch quite close to the ground. Plant fibers along with strips of dry leaf and sometimes bark are held together with spiders' webs. It is usually lined with very fine fibers from seeding plants and frequently decorated on the outside with other local plant debris. The female incubates her two eggs for two weeks, taking another three weeks before the young fledge.

Cuban Emerald

Chlorostilbon ricordii

Male: 4½" (11½cm)

Female: 4" (10cm)

Distributed throughout Cuba, the Isle of Pines, and the northern Bahama Islands, where it occurs throughout the lowlands, the Cuban Emerald does, however, occasionally appear as a vagrant in the southernmost tip of Florida, USA. It does not seem associated with any particular type of habitat being found in both dry open countryside as well as humid forest, although it seems more prevalent in areas containing low shrubs. It is also common close to human habitation in yards, parks, and plantations where a succession of flowering shrubs are present. Nectar is a main food source along with insects and small spiders caught either by gleaning or hawking.

Males have a shining bronze-green plumage with the throat and breast iridescent green and undertail coverts light gray to white. The area covering the forehead and crown often has a darker and duller appearance. There is a small white spot behind the eye. The dark-colored forked tail has a metallic bronze sheen and the wings are black but tinged green. The very slightly curved bill is mainly black, with the lower mandible showing signs of red on the underside toward the base. Females are very similar although they lack the iridescent green underparts, having a buff white throat and breast which becomes iridescent green at the flanks. She has a larger and longer white spot behind the eye, a less forked tail sometimes tipped white, and white undertail coverts.

Breeding takes place throughout the year. A low site, frequently located amongst vines but also in the outer branches of low trees is chosen for the cup-shaped nest; a construction of fine plant fibers, moss and thin bark strips bound together with spiders' webs. Externally it is decorated with tiny pieces of lichen or bark fragments. The female incubates two eggs for just over two weeks and the young fledge around three weeks later.

Puerto Rican Emerald

Chlorostilbon maugaeus

Male: 3½" (9cm)

Female: 3" (7½cm)

The Puerto Rican or Antillean Emerald as it is also known, can be found throughout the island from mountaintops down to the coast. Its preferred habitats seem to be associated with woodland, trees, and large shrubs, be they forests, open woodland, or plantations. A very wide range of flowering trees and shrubs are exploited for nectar and shrubs, and tree canopies are gleaned for insects and spiders.

The upperparts, nape, crown, forehead, lower belly, and undertail coverts are a dark iridescent green contrasting with the bright iridescent blue-green throat patch. The forked tail is dark blue with a brilliant sheen and the wings black. The smaller female differs in plumage apart from the green upperparts nape, crown, and forehead. This coloration continues down her back and through the tail coverts to halfway along the tail when it blends into a black-brown band before ending at the white tipped tail feathers. Her tail is only slightly forked.

Although nesting takes place throughout the year, the main breeding season is from late February through to May. Tiny cup-shaped nests are constructed in low shrubs and trees using mainly plant fibers and a lining of plant down. The outside is frequently disguised with small pieces of lichen and leaf. The female incubates her two eggs for a little over two weeks and it is a further three weeks before the young fledge.

Fiery-throated Hummingbird

Panterpe insignis

4¼" (11cm)

Also called the Irazu Hummingbird, there are two races—both preferring the montane forests and cloudforests of Costa Rica. They are also frequently seen outside the forest, around the edges and in clearings, as well as in in areas of grassland where dense pockets of trees remain. The nominate race *P. i. insignis* is found from central Costa Rica eastward to the border with Panama, whereas *P. i. eisenmanni* remains in the north. They have a wide variety of flowering food plants from which to obtain nectar including trees, shrubs, epiphytes, vines, and herbs. Besides hovering to feed they are known to pierce holes in the base of longer blooms or to make use of holes made by other birds or insects to obtain the nectar. Insects and flies are also taken in flight by hawking.

Both males and females have similar plumage, the upperparts being a brilliant dark green, becoming glittering dark blue on the forehead and crown. The tail coverts are graded from green to dark blue and then into a blue-black rather square tail. The lores are black and an area of greenish-black extends around the ear coverts and over the nape. There is a small white spot behind the eye. The throat is a mixture of brilliant iridescent spots of color from an orange-red at the center grading through yellow to bright green at the sides. Below the throat is an equally brilliant patch of emerald green and purple being surrounded below and at the sides by bright green. The upper mandible is black and lower mandible pink. The northern Costa Rican race differs in being smaller and having more blue on the rump and breast.

Breeding takes place between late summer and January when a bulky nest is attached to a twig some ten feet (three meters) from the ground. Plant down and moss are intermixed with spiders' webs and decorated with lichen and treefern pieces. Only two eggs are laid, taking some two and a half weeks to incubate.

Coppery-headed Emerald

Elvira cupreiceps

3" (7½cm)

This small hummingbird breeds in a relatively confined area of the Costa Rican highlands but then descends into the lowlands. It prefers the cooler and wetter forests during the breeding season from October to March, but it can also be found in more open country with copses and scattered mature trees as well as secondary growth, plantations, and shrubbery. Nectar from flowering trees, shrubs and epiphytes go toward its diet along with many insects and spiders gleaned from foliage as well as flies caught by hawking.

The male's plumage is distinctly coppery colored over the crown and upper-tail coverts and bronze-green over the nape, back, and wing coverts. The forehead is iridescent yellow-bronze and throat, neck, and breast bright iridescent green. In some areas the male has a purple spot around the middle of the breast. Vent and undertail coverts are white. The inner tail feathers are a gray-bronze and the white outer tail feathers tipped with gray spots. It has an obviously decurved black bill showing a little pink at the base of the lower mandible. The female is duller and greener with off-white underparts having green spots at the flanks.

Breeding is from late October through to March when a nest is constructed low down in a shrub from soft plant fibers. The compact cup-shape is held together with spiders' webs and decorated with moss, lichen, and scales of treefern. Apart from the clutch size of two eggs there is little other breeding information.

Stripe-tailed Hummingbird

Eupherusa eximia

4" (10cm)

The three races of this species are from three separate areas of the highlands from southern Mexico eastward to western Panama. *E. e. nelsoni* is the more westerly, being concentrated in the mountains west of Vera Cruz. The nominate race, *E. e. eximia*, ranges from western Chiapas through Guatemala and Honduras into central Nicaragua. *E. e. egregia* is from the mountains of Costa Rica eastward and into Western Panama. They are fairly common within their range and mainly sedentary, with only small altitudinal movements before and after breeding. Mainly a forest dweller, keeping to the edges and canopy it often ventures out into more open habitat especially in association with riverine habitat where pockets of dense shrub and secondary growth exist. It searches out flowers from a variety of trees, shrubs, and epiphytes to obtain nectar; often piercing the flower base in the longer bell-shaped blooms. Spiders and insects are gleaned from foliage and flies caught in mid-air.

Males have both upper and underparts green, with a bronze sheen on the head and back, and a spotted iridescence on the breast. The slightly rounded tail is blackish-green, the two outer feathers being white at the base and tipped black with black edges to the outer webs. The wing has black primaries and reddish secondaries. The short, straight bill is black. Females are a buff gray over the underparts with green spotting at the flanks. The red coloring of the secondaries is less extensive and not so bright, and the black outer edges of the tail feathers are much narrower and often missing altogether.

Breeding starts as the wet season is coming to an end when a nest site is chosen, often close to water but within the seclusion of dense woodland. The nest is constructed of very fine plant fibers and pieces of moss and lichen held together with spiders' webs and further decorated with lichen and moss. Little other breeding information is available.

Broad-billed Hummingbird

Cynanthus latirostris

3½–4" (9–10cm)

There are five races of this species, the most northerly, *C. l. magicus,* being found from southern Arizona and southwest New Mexico southward into the mountains of Nayarit in western central Mexico. Off the coast of Mexico, west of Nayarit, lie the islands Las Tres Marias where *C. l. lawrencei* or Lawrence's Hummingbird is found. *C. l. latirostris* ranges from the northeast Mexican coast down through Tamaulipas and San Luis Potosi and into Vera Cruz. To the west of Central Mexico, *C. l. propinquus* is spread through Michoacan up to Guanajuato. *C. l. doubledayi*, known also as Doubleday's Hummingbird, is found along the Pacific coastal area of southern Mexico, taking in Chiapas, Oaxaca, and Guerrero. The southern races are resident, but birds from the northerly races migrate southward after breeding. The northerly races, particularly those into the United States, are frequently found in ravines, canyons, and deserts where there is an abundance of plant growth—especially mesquite and sycamore—whereas in Mexico they are more likely to be found in dry shrubby and open areas with scattered trees right down to the coast. Food sources include nectar from flowering shrubs, cacti, and succulents as well as spiders and insects gleaned from foliage.

Like many hummingbirds it looks very dark from a distance, however, the males are iridescent green on the crown, nape, and back, with a blue or violet-blue throat. The underparts are a shining bronze-green leading into buff-white undertail coverts. The notched tail is blue-black. Females have dull yellow-green upperparts leading into a blue-green tail with a black sub-terminal band and a white tip. Her underparts are gray-buff as are her ear coverts. To the rear of the ear coverts is a white stripe. She has a black upper mandible and red lower while the male's bill is red tipped black. Males of the race *C. l. doubledayi* have generally darker plumage with beautiful iridescent dark turquoise foreheads and black undertail coverts. *C. l. magicus* has a green throat, whereas *C. l. lawrencei* has turquoise.

Breeding takes place from April to September in the north of the range but can start much earlier in the south. The untidy cup-shaped nest of plant fibers and spiders' webs, decorated with pieces of leaf and bark, is usually sited low down on top of a horizontal branch. Two eggs are incubated by the female for two to three weeks, the young fledging about three weeks later.

Blue-headed Hummingbird

Cyanophaia bicolor

4½" (11cm)

Another common name for this species which occurs in Martinique and Dominica is Wagler's Woodnymph. It is sedentary and found mainly in more mountainous terrain, especially within primary rainforest and at forest edges abutting rivers and streams. Not a common species, it is susceptible to the ravages of weather, particularly hurricanes, which often devastate the area. Populations of the species therefore fluctuate considerably. It takes nectar from a wide variety of flowering plants, from trees to herbs as well as foraging for insects and spiders amongst foliage and hawking for flies in the air.

The male is identified by his iridescent violet-blue head, including the chin and throat, and the rest of the iridescent body plumage is all-green apart from dark blue upper tail coverts. The flight feathers are black and the forked tail blue-black. His straight bill is all black apart from the base of the lower mandible which is reddish-pink. The female is quite different having all bright bronze-green upperparts including the forehead and crown right down to the top half of the tail. Her central tail feathers are tipped dark blue, and the outers are a finely tipped white with a dark blue sub-terminal band. Underparts are pale buff-gray, becoming bronze-green at the flanks.

The short breeding season is from March until May, when a nest site is chosen—usually fairly close to the ground on thin branches or even on ferns. The small cup-shaped nest is constructed from soft, silky plant fibers, sometimes incorporating spiders' webs but usually decorated with pieces of leaf and other plant debris. The female incubates the two eggs for a little over two weeks and the young take some three weeks to fledge.

Purple-crowned Woodnymph

Thalurania colombica

Male: 4" (10cm)

Female: 3½" (9cm)

Very slight variations in color have given rise to this species also having the name of Violet Woodnymph and Violet-crowned Woodnymph, although races occurring in Guatemala and Honduras (*T. c. townsendi*) and Colombia into northwest Venezuela (*T. c. colombica*) are also have different names: Blue-crowned Woodnymph and Colombian Woodnymph respectively. Two other races are recognized, *T. c. venusta* coming from eastern Nicaragua through Costa Rica and into central Panama and *T. c. rostrifera* only found in the far northwest of Venezuela. They are all thought to be sedentary although dispersion occurs after breeding and there is movement coinciding with food availability.

This hummingbird is more of a forest dweller, keeping to the shaded areas of humid forest and forest edges and avoiding more open habitat. However, it can be found in shrubby yards shaded by trees or in plantations and secondary growth.

This species regularly hawks for insects in "flycatcher fashion" choosing a prominent twig below the tree canopy from which to hunt and it will also glean amongst the foliage for insects and spider prey. Nectar is taken from a broad range of flowering plants, in particular small shrubs and trees as well as epiphytes but seldom outside the tree canopy.

Males have, on their forehead, crown, and belly, a purple-violet with patches of similar coloration at the bend of the wing and across the upper-back. The deeply forked tail is also a dark violet color. The nape, lower back, and rump are a bronze-green, sometimes tinged violet; the wings black with a bluish sheen, and the throat and upper breast iridescent bright green. The straight bill is black. Females are bright green including the upperparts, wing coverts, and the flanks extending into the belly. The remainder of the underparts are gray-buff becoming darker in the center of the belly. Her almost straight-cut tail is bronze-green at the coverts becoming blue-black at the end, the three outer-tail feathers being tipped white.

It chooses the drier weather in which to breed. The small cup-shaped nest is usually placed low down on top of a branch and hidden beneath a large leaf. Plant down and spiders' webs intermixed with pieces of tree-fern, moss, and lichen are used in its construction. No other reliable information is available on breeding.

Fork-tailed Woodnymph

Thalurania furcata

3–4" (7½–10cm)

This mainly sedentary species is very widely distributed throughout most of South America north of the Tropic of Capricorn and east of the Andes, apart from the northeastern coast of Brazil. At present most of the 13 recognized races are fairly common but deforestation in many areas is giving cause for concern. It is found in a wide range of habitats but particularly in humid forest and along forest edges. In places it can be found in plantations and secondary woodland and also in gardens and more open areas. Its favorite sources of nectar include the flowers of many trees and shrubs as well as vines, epiphytes, and the larger herbs such as heliconia. It also gleans for insects and spiders and hawks for small flies.

Males of this species all have dark, dull green upperparts with the nape and crown a brown-green. The underparts are a dark blue, sometimes tinged violet as is the narrow collar band across the upper back. The throat and face are an iridescent bright green. The forked tail is a blackish-blue with dark gray-blue undertail coverts showing whiter edges. The lower belly and vent are gray, but in one race, *T. f. balzani*, the vent and undertail coverts appear almost all white. The flight feathers are black with bronze-green wing coverts and a violet-blue patch on the bend of the wing. The straight bill is black and varies slightly in length amongst the races. Females have slightly brighter green upperparts becoming tinged with a dull brown on the crown. Underparts are a dull buff-gray and the tail feathers blue-black with the three outers tipped white. The various races are individually recognized by slight variations in plumage coloration but remain around the same size, apart from *T. f. furcatoides* from the lower Amazon region of eastern Brazil which is slightly larger. As would be expected, there is intermixing of the races where they meet at their boundaries and plumages take on traits from each other.

It is thought that breeding takes place from April to October but there is little other evidence other than the state of the bird's plumage.

White-chinned Sapphire

Hylocharis cyanus

3–3½" (7½–9cm)

The five races of the White-chinned Sapphire are widespread in their distribution, preferring forest edges and damp woodland to the arid regions. They are more of a lowland species occurring in some places at the coast but more often at slightly higher elevations from 600ft (200m) to just over 3,000ft (1,000m) above sea level. The nominate race *H. c. cyanus* is resident along the eastern coast of Brazil from Pernambuco to São Paulo where it intermixes with *H. C. griseiventris,* which ranges further south to Buenos Aires in Argentina. *H. c. viridiventris* extends its range from northern Colombia eastward through the Guianas and into northern Brazil. *H. c. conversa* is found in a broad strip covering eastern Bolivia, through north Paraguay and into southwestern Brazil and *H. c. rostrata* covers a large area of the Amazonas. It is quite often found close to human habitation and readily accepts secondary growth, clearings, plantations, parks, and gardens including open areas with scattered trees. It is a nectar feeder also taking numerous insects and spiders which it gleans from foliage.

Upperparts are a brilliant iridescent yellow-green which blend into a bronze-red at the rump. The tail is blue-black. The forehead and cheeks leading down to the neck and round to the lower throat are a bright violet-blue. Below this the underparts are gray-green at the center of the belly becoming greener at the lower belly and flanks. The chin and upper-throat are white to off-white. The straight bill is red tipped black in the male although some have darker upper mandibles. The female is very similar but lacks the violet-blue coloring on the head. She has slightly brighter green coloration with an all-green forehead, crown, and ear-coverts. Her underparts are greenish with patches of buff-gray to white in the center of the belly, throat, and undertail coverts.

Breeding takes place at almost any time of the year and a cup-shaped nest is built on top of a branch anywhere up to about ten feet (three meters) above the ground. The construction is mainly of plant fibers interlaced with spiders' webs and decorated with small pieces of lichen. The female incubates her two eggs for two weeks and the young fledge some three to four weeks later.

Rufous-tailed Hummingbird

Amazilia tzacatl

3¼–4½" (8–11 cm)

This little hummingbird is also known as the Rieffer's or the Escudo Hummingbird and there are four sub-species. The nominate race *A. t. tzacatl* is found from the central and eastern side of Mexico south eastward to central Panama. *A. t. handleyi* is the largest and inhabits the island of Escudo de Veraguas off northwest Panama. The range of *A. t. fuscicaudata* covers western Venezuela through north to western Colombia and *A. t. jucunda* covers southwest Colombia through western Ecuador.

Throughout the range it is found in a huge variety of habitats from beaches and mangrove on the coast up to open forests 8,000 ft (2,500m) up in the Andes. It seems to prefer clearings and forest edges, whether they are cultivated plantations or evergreen forest, but is seldom seen in dense growth. On the coast they are often found in open areas containing shrubby thickets. It feeds from ground level to the tree canopy often hanging on adjacent foliage or petals to get at flower nectar. It also gleans for spiders and insects along the surface of branches and amongst leafy foliage. Like many other hummingbirds it makes use of the holes pierced into the base of flowers by the Bananaquit (*Coereba flaveola*) to reach the nectar. Where the availability of its food sources is relatively stable the birds are more sedentary but in the drier hilly areas there is likely to be some altitudinal migration, as food becomes scarce.

Upperparts and upper belly vary from a metallic bronze-green to a golden-green, iridescence creating colors of turquoise blue and yellow mainly on the throat. The lower belly varies from pale gray to brown-gray. The tail is a pale-chestnut. The female is very similar to the male, differing mainly at the throat where the plumage appears more mottled and at the belly, which is white. The red bill is straight, usually with a near black tip but the upper mandible can sometimes show black throughout.

Breeding can take place at almost any time of the year but there are regional variations. The nest is more likely to be built on a horizontal branch some six to 12 feet (two to four meters) above the ground but occasionally other sites are chosen. Plant fibers are formed into a cup-shape and bound together with spiders' webs before being decorated with lichens and pieces of dead leaf. The female incubates her two eggs for just over two weeks, the young fledging a round three weeks later.

Amazilia Hummingbird

Amazilia amazilia

3½–4½" (9–11cm)

Four races of the Amazilia Hummingbird are recognized. The bird illustrated is Dumerill's Hummingbird (*Amazilia amazilia dumerilii*), which lives west of the Andes from northern Peru through western Ecuador as well as in areas of southeast Ecuador. The other three races are found west of the Andes in Peru. Quite common in cultivated areas and yards and often observed in towns and cities, it can also be located in more natural habitat of open dry desert areas with scattered scrub and thorn forest from sub-montane regions and often right down to the coast. Occasionally it is also seen in forested areas. It is generally thought to be resident but there is often a dispersal of birds after breeding to different altitudes. Besides feeding on nectar, it will also forage for small insects and spiders.

Breeding can take place at almost any time throughout the year when a cup-shaped nest of fine plant fibers bound together with spiders' webs is constructed on the top of a flat horizontal branch. Nests can also be located in dense bushes for protection where adverse wet weather conditions persist. Two eggs are laid which are incubated by the female for up to 18 days. Fledging takes place after a further three weeks.

This species has dark to yellow-green upperparts blending into rufous tail feathers on the lower back. The red bill is straight with a dark, almost black tip; the dark area on the lower mandible often extending half way along the bill. The throat is a mottled dark turquoise-green. The breast and belly are light chestnut brown becoming very pale at the vent. Females are very similar often having paler underparts particularly on the lower belly. The subspecies *A. a. dumerilii* and *A. a. leucophaea* have a few white chin markings and patches of white below the green throat and on the belly.

Cinnamon Hummingbird

Amazilia rutila

4" (10cm)

The nominate race of the Cinnamon Hummingbird, *A. r. rutila* is found in the southwestern coastal states of Mexico from Oaxaca to Jalisco. *A. r. diluta* ranges northward through Nayarit and Sinaloa and *A. r. graysoni* is confined to the islands Las Tres Marias just off Nayarit. The fourth race, *A. r. corallirostris*, extends from Yucatan in Mexico down into Chiapas, and then along the Pacific coast through much of Guatemala, Honduras, and Nicaragua and into Costa Rica. Although preferring the drier tropical habitat, the Cinnamon Hummingbird can be found in a wide variety of environments and especially more open forest. It is quite common at lower elevations especially areas of secondary growth and may often be found close to human habitation. Its main diet is nectar from flowering trees and shrubs as well as vines and other plants. Insects and spiders are also taken and flies are often caught by hawking.

The cinnamon-rufous underparts are very evident both in males and females of all races although there is some variation in color density. Most show a pale to white patch at the vent. The upperparts are bright green over the head and bends of the wing, becoming golden-bronze over the back. The very slightly notched tail is rufous at the base with green-bronze to purple tips. The flight feathers are black and the male's straight bill is pinkish-red with a black tip. The female, generally with slightly paler underparts and a brownish chin, has a mainly black bill with red at the base of the lower mandible.

Breeding can take place throughout the year when a cup-shaped nest of fine plant fibers held together with spiders' webs and decorated with tree-fern pieces is built on a branch in a secluded shrub or low tree. Two eggs are incubated by the female for a little over two weeks.

Violet-crowned Hummingbird

Agyrtria violiceps

4" (10cm)

Often called the Azurecrown and earlier known as this Salvin's Hummingbird this species was previously grouped with the Amazilia genus of hummingbirds and given the scientific name of *Amazilia verticalis*. Two races are now recognized, the nominate *A. v. violiceps* coming from southwest Mexico whereas *A. v. ellioti* ranges from central Mexico northward into southwestern USA. As they are partial migrants, it is not unusual for them to wander into western USA to southeast Arizona and southern California.

This largish hummingbird is quite common throughout its range but more often found in the south. Dry open scrubland with sycamore and agaves is a regular habitat as are more open pine and pine-oak woodlands and forest edges, but they frequently come close to human habitation and into parks and yards. Birds migrating into the USA are frequently found in canyons where there is water and lush vegetation. They take nectar from flowering trees and tall plants with a particular liking for the agave. Insects and spiders are either hawked in the air or gleaned from high in the tree-tops.

A medium sized hummingbird, the male is usually recognized by its gleaming all-white underparts and violet-blue crown, nape, and forehead. The upperparts and flanks are a bronze-tinged olive-green, becoming more purple on the upper-tail coverts and central tail feathers. The straight bill is red tipped with black. Females are very similar but with the nape and the back of the neck tinged turquoise.

Breeding is usually from April to August with nests being built high in trees in the north of the range but often low down in the south. The cup-shaped nest is constructed of plant fibers and down intermixed with lichens and bound together with spiders' webs on top of a horizontal branch. The female incubates her two eggs for about two weeks, the young fledging some three weeks later.

Steely-vented Hummingbird

Saucerrottei saucerrottei

4¼" (11cm)

Also known as the Blue-vented Hummingbird as well as Saucerotte's Hummingbird, this species was once grouped with the Amazilia genus. Four races are now recognized, *S. s. saucerrottei* ranging through the drier lowland areas of north and west Colombia. The western Venezuelan race, *S. s. braccata,* keeps more to the foothills at around 6,500ft (2,000m). *S. s. warscewiczi* is also found in the far north of Colombia but extends its range just into Venezuela. *S. s. hoffmanni* is isolated in the south and southwest of Nicaragua and the western half of Costa Rica.

This species keeps mainly to the lowlands and foothills preferring more open habitat such as savannas and open dry forest with shrubby exuberances. Areas of scrub, forest edges, and, frequently, yards and gardens are exploited for nectar from flowering trees and shrubs. Epiphytes and vines are also used along with many of the low-growing plants. Spiders and insects are often gleaned from foliage.

Although at first appearing to be one of the more mundane colored hummingbirds, the general overall green appearance of this bird has outstanding iridescence, particularly on the breast in certain lights. The male's slightly forked tail is blue-black, as are the upper tail coverts. The undertail coverts are a steely-blue often tinged green. He has a straight bill, the upper mandible being black and the lower being orange-red with a black tip. The female has a similar appearance but shows white mottling on the throat and brownish undertail coverts. Her tail is notched rather than forked.

There seems to be no particular breeding season for this species, with nests being found throughout the year. A typical nest site is on the top of a horizontal branch well off the ground in a small tree. Cup-shaped nests are constructed of fine plant fibers and spiders' webs and camouflaged externally with pieces of lichen. It is known that the female incubates only two eggs and they hatch in about two weeks but no other reliable breeding information is available.

Snowcap

Microchera albocoronata

2½" (6½cm)

This tiny hummingbird is also known as the White-crowned Hummingbird with two races being recognized. The nominate and darker colored race, *M. a. albocoronata,* is found on the lower hillsides of western and central Panama. *M. a. parvirostris* ranges well to the west along a northern hillside coastal belt from west Panama through Costa Rica and Nicaragua and just into southeastern Honduras. Although preferring natural wet forest and forest boundaries where it exploits flowering trees and shrubs, it often ventures out into nearby hedgerows searching out small flowers and gleaning insects and spiders. It can often be seen along forest edges hawking for aerial insects.

Easily recognized within its range by its brilliant white crown, the male has bright iridescent purple-red upperparts becoming more bronze-colored on the central tail feathers. The undertail coverts are white and outer tail feathers are whitish at the base becoming darker toward the black tips. The underparts are blackish with a bright violet sheen over the breast becoming bronze to green at the throat. The short straight bill is black. Females retain the snowy-white cap although it is smaller than the male's. They have gleaming green upperparts and gray-white underparts. The rump and tail appear reddish-bronze, the tail having a darker sub-terminal band.

Nests are usually constructed on top of a low branch from very fine plant fibers and tree-fern pieces all bound together with spiders' webs and decorated with moss and lichen. No reliable information is available on breeding details.

Blue-throated Hummingbird

Lampornis clemenciae

5" (13cm)

Another of the species regularly found in the far southwestern United States and into Mexico, but normally in mountain ranges at altitudes above 5,000ft (1,500m) and even as high as 10,000ft (3,000m). *L. c. clemenciae* ranges into southwest Texas southward through the center of Mexico as far south as Oaxaca. *L. c. bessophilus* has a more northwesterly distribution and is found in a band from the south of Arizona and southwest New Mexico southward through west Chihuahua and east Sonora. It is a bird of the drier mountain slopes and canyons often found in riverine habitats with a plentiful growth of low flowering plants from which it can obtain nectar. It also takes a wide variety of insects and spiders. Artificial feeding, particularly in the United States, has encouraged unnaturally large congregations which could not be supported by natural means. As a medium sized hummingbird it does exert a certain amount of dominance over other hummingbirds at feeding stations. There is some altitudinal migration of birds in the south of the range and many of the more northerly birds migrate south for the winter.

The male has a very attractive bright iridescent blue gorget contrasting with buffish-gray underparts and brown-gray ear coverts. The ear coverts are bordered to the rear by a broad white stripe and often there appears a short thin white moustachial stripe. The upperparts are a bronze-green, showing lighter green across the top of the back. Bronze-colored tail coverts overlay a blackish-blue rounded tail, tipped white on the outer feathers. The wings and slightly decurved bill are black. Females are a little duller and almost identical apart from having all buffish-gray underparts including the throat.

The breeding season is geared to flowering seasons and in the USA occurs from May to early summer. Sites are chosen for protection from above, such as thick foliage or rock above a crevice. The nest, a cup-shaped structure, is built from fine plant fibers, moss, and lichens and is held together with spiders' webs. The outside is often decorated with pieces of lichen, twig, and bark fragments. The female incubates her two eggs for two and a half weeks, the young fledging almost a month later.

Variable Mountain-gem

Lampornis castaneoventris

4½" (11½cm)

As might be expected with the name "Variable" there are several different forms of this species, all recognized as different races, but there is debate as to whether they should be classed as different species. They all occur in a relatively small area from southern Nicaragua through Costa Rica and into western Panama where they inhabit mainly tree-tops and woodland edges of mountain forests. In more open habitat they keep to shrubby areas and may also be found in plantations and agricultural land. Their diet consists of nectar from a wide variety of flowering plants; the males seeming to prefer flowers of epiphytes within the forest canopy whereas females feed lower down on flowering shrubs. Numerous insects and spiders are also taken by gleaning through foliage.

The males of the five races are recognized mainly through the color of the iridescent gorget and tail. The nominate race, the White-throated Mountain-gem (*L. c. castaneoventris*) from western Panama has a brilliant-white gorget and blue-black tail, glittering bronze-green upperparts and upper breast with belly and vent being buffish-gray. Very similar is the Grey-tailed Mountain-gem (*L. c. cinereicauda*) from southern Costa Rica which has a brown-gray tail, turquoise blue forehead, and more wide-spread green on the breast. The Purple-throated Mountain-gem (*L. c. calolaemus*) from Costa Rica is similar to *L. c. cinereicauda* but has a purple gorget and dark blue tail. *L. c. pectoralis*, also similar, has a purple-blue gorget, turquoise-blue forehead, and almost all glittering dark green underparts. The ear coverts are black to dark green bordered at the rear by a white stripe leading from the rear and top of the eye down to the neck. The straight bill is all black and feet a reddish-brown. Females of all races are very similar, having all green upperparts and cinnamon-red underparts. The tail is bronze-green with a blackish sub-terminal band and white tip to the outer tail feathers.

This species chooses the rainy season in which to breed selecting a low site on a branch at the edge of a clearing on which to build its cup-shaped nest. Fine plant fibers and down along with pieces of tree-fern are bound together with spiders' webs and then decorated externally with lichens and moss. The female incubates her two eggs for between two and three weeks and the young fledge almost a month later.

Above right: **A male White-throated Mountain-gem.**

Below right: **Female Purple-throated Mountain-gem.**

White-eared Hummingbird

Basilinna leucotis

4" (10cm)

This highland species consists of three races: *B. l. pygmaea,* which ranges from southern Nicaragua through Honduras, eastern Guatemala, and north into El Salvador; *B. l. leucotis*, the nominate, extends through Guatemala northward into central Mexico; and *B. l. borealis* is found in northern Mexico. The northern race has a tendency to migrate northward in the spring occasionally being found in southern Arizona and Texas, USA. Highland pine-oak and pine-evergreen forests are its favorite habitats particularly where there is an understorey of flowering shrubby growth. It feeds on nectar but also hawks and gleans for insects and spiders.

The male's upperparts are mainly green with a rufous tinge on the nape, lower back, and upper tail coverts. The forehead, crown, and chin are iridescent violet and the frontal ear coverts black, contrasting with a white stripe extending from above and behind the eye down to the neck. Immediately below the chin, the iridescent green of the gorget extends downward, blending into a grayish-green lower belly and vent. The very slightly forked tail is green with the outer feathers edged black and the straight bill is red at the base with a black tip. The female has similarly colored ear coverts and upperparts, but she lacks the violet coloration on the head. She has an all black upper mandible and the forehead and crown is bronze-colored. The underparts are off white, marked with iridescent green spots. Her greenish tail has bronze edges to the outer-tail feathers and white tips.

This species probably nests throughout the year. The cup-shaped nest is usually on a branch, sometimes on the top of an old nest, and constructed from plant fibers and leaf fragments decorated with lichen. Two eggs are incubated by the female for just over two weeks and fledging can take up to four weeks longer.

Fawn-breasted Brilliant

Heliodoxa rubinoides

5" (13cm)

This species has several other common names including Lilac-breasted Brilliant, Lilac-throated Hummingbird, and Penny-throated Hummingbird. Found on the slopes of the Andes through Colombia, Ecuador, and Peru this very dark hummingbird is separated into three races. The nominate race, *H. r. rubinoides,* resides in the central and eastern Andes of Colombia. To the west of the Andes through Colombia and Ecuador *H. r. aequatorialis* may be found and back on the east of the Andes through Ecuador and into Peru is *H. r. cervinigularis*. Nowhere is it common, keeping mainly to altitudes of 5,500-6,000ft (1,700–1,800m) except after breeding when it may disperse to both higher and lower altitudes. It inhabits particularly wet and humid forests being found particularly at the edges and often wandering further afield into agricultural and urban environments. Although it is often seen flycatching for aerial insects, its main diet is nectar from flowering trees and shrubs.

The upperparts are very dark iridescent bronze-green with blackish-bronze wings and brown tinged wing coverts. The underparts are warm brown becoming dark green at the flanks. The male of the nominate race has a dark green throat with a small iridescent purple patch just below. The male of the race *H. r. cervinigularis* has a smaller and less dense iridescent throat patch.

Breeding takes place in the latter quarter of the year in Ecuador but in the first few months of the year in Colombia. Apart from the fact that the female incubates two eggs, no other breeding details are available.

Green-crowned Brilliant

Heliodoxa jacula

male:5" (13cm)

female:4½" (11½cm)

Also known as the Green-fronted Brilliant, there are three separate races of this species. *H. j. jacula*, the nominate, is found in Central and north Colombia as far west as its border with Panama. In the far soutwest of Colombia and into western Ecuador *H. j. jamesoni* is resident. *H. j. henryi* can be located in Costa Rica and western Panama where it undertakes an altitudinal migration down into the lowlands after breeding. The preferred habitat seems to be in areas of wet and cloudforest of the foothills and mountains that border on more open countryside. Here they are found in the understorey where they search out the long, bell-shaped flowers to which they are well adapted. They are also attracted to the flowers of shrubs especially heliconia as well as the flowering epiphytes. This hummingbird not only hovers to feed but frequently takes the easy way out and perches on the plant itself. It will also glean foliage for spiders and insects as well as hawking.

The very dark color of this hummingbird is very deceptive until it gets into bright light when, in the males, the dark blue-green becomes dazzlingly brilliant. This color predominates over the head and down the throat and upper breast apart from the white spot behind the eye and a tiny patch of iridescent violet-blue between the lower neck and breast. The lores and a very small triangular patch above the base of the bill can both appear black at times. The upperparts from the back downward are tinged bronze including the central tail feathers. The outer feathers of the deeply forked tail are bluish-black. The female is not as brilliant having whitish underparts spotted green; the outer tail feathers tipped white and a whitish malar stripe. The races differ slightly in plumage; the male *H. j. jamesoni* is less brilliant generally and has a short greenish tail whereas the male of *H. j. henryi* is brighter with a totally blue-black tail.

To date there is little breeding information available for this species.

Magnificent Hummingbird

Eugenes fulgens

4½–5" (11–13cm)

This species is known by several other common names, in particular Rivoli's Hummingbird. To others it is the Admiral Hummingbird but the sub-species *E. f. spectablis,* which occurs in Costa Rica and Panama, account for the names of Costa Rica or Panama Hummingbird. The nominate race *E. f. fulgens* occurs from the very southwest of the United States through Mexico and Central America and into northeast Nicaragua. Although the Central American populations are considered to be sedentary, there is thought to be movement of some north Mexican birds into the USA for the breeding season. It is primarily a bird of the hills but seldom found above 8,000ft (2,500m) and usually only migrates to below 5,000ft (1,500m) when the weather turns cold.

It relies for food on nectar bearing flowering plants as well as small flies, beetles, and spiders.

Males have very dark green upperparts and green underparts becoming very dark, almost black, on the lower belly. The gorget is iridescent green and the crown iridescent purple. There is a very dark green-black eyestripe which accentuates the small white spot behind the eye. They have robust, straight black bills and a bronze-colored tail. The female's plumage is more mundane, lacking iridescence on the gorget and the purple crown. Her upperparts are an overall dark-green and underparts grayish-buff with the wings and tail appearing more bronze-green.

Resident birds in Central America have a breeding season extending from November until July but others delay the start of breeding until May. Detailed information on nesting is limited, however, nests are usually found well off the ground on high tree branches. They are a cup-shaped construction of fine plant fibers lined with plant down and covered externally with pieces of lichen and tiny shreds of bark. The female incubates her two eggs for over two weeks.

Right: **Male.**

Below: **Female.**

Shining Sunbeam

Aglaeactis cupripennis

4¾–5" (12–13cm)

Also known as the Copper-winged Hummingbird, there are two recognized races, the nominate *A. c. cupripennis* being found in the northern Andes from Colombia to central Peru. The other, *A. c. caumatonotus,* also in Peru, occurs to the south almost as far as Lake Titicaca. This species prefers the more open páramo, a predominantly grassland with scattered trees and shrubs, as well as the drier mountain ridges, slopes, and cloudforest, usually where trees are present and normally above 8,000ft (2,500m). It is a resident species, although it will descend to lower elevations in inclement weather.

While it takes aerial insects by hawking, its main diet consists of nectar from flowering vines, shrubs, trees, and bromeliads.

The Shining Sunbeam is by far the most widely distributed and fairly common throughout its range, whereas the other "sunbeams" have restricted ranges. Although of similar plumage to the others of the Agleactis genus, being characterized by their brilliant iridescent lower-back and rump on an otherwise mundane colored plumage, it has much lighter rufous-brown underparts. Their iridescent back patch is almost "rainbow-colored," contrasting with a dark-brown wings, mantle, and crown. The tail is also dark brown becoming rufous at the lower tail coverts. The short, straight bill is black. Females are very similar but the iridescent back patch is either less bright or replaced by brown.

It is known to nest at all times of the year depending on location. It usually chooses a site high in a tree often attaching its nest to an epiphyte. Mosses, lichens, plant fibers, and hairs are bound together to form a cup-shaped nest which is decorated externally with small pieces of lichen, leaves, and bark. Two eggs are laid taking the female around 18 days to incubate. It is almost four weeks before the young fledge.

Collared Inca

Coeligena torquata

5¾" (14½cm)

Also known as the White-cravat Hummingbird, it is easy to see why. All six races of this large hummingbird, both males and females, sporting an immaculate broad white collar. They are all fairly sedentary inhabitants of edges and clearings of humid montane forests of the Andes. The nominate race, *C. t. torquata* ranges from northern Peru and Eastern Ecuador up through Colombia and eastward into western Venezuela. *C. t. eisenmanni* is from southern Peru, *C. t. insectivora* from central Peru, and *C. t. margaretae* from northern Peru. Further north in Ecuador, *C. t. fulgidigula* is found to the west of the Andes and in northwest Venezuela in the Andes south of Lake Maracaibo is *C. t. conradii*. They keep below the canopy searching for nectar from flowering trees and shrubs. Insects and spiders are gleaned from foliage and flies are caught by hawking.

All races have predominantly iridescent green upperparts, bellies, and central tail feathers; the color varying in darkness between races. Outer tail feathers of the forked tail are white at the base with shining green tips. Apart from *C. t. conradii*, which has an all green head, males have black foreheads and napes and green chins. The nominate race and males of *C. t. fulgidigula* have purplish-blue crown spots and all have small white spots to the rear of the eye. They have long and straight black bills. Females lack the green chins, the color being replaced by dirty-white, sometimes tinged buffish-orange, plumage spotted with green.

Although breeding information is rather scant, nests have occasionally been located on cliff-faces, hidden amongst ferns. The cup-shaped construction is built mainly from plant fibers and fern pieces. Like most hummingbird species, the two eggs are incubated only by the female.

Sword-billed Hummingbird

Ensifera ensifera

6¾–9" (17–23cm)

This hummingbird deserves its name, its black slightly upturned bill, shaped like a sword, has a length of around four inches (ten centimeters), about half the bird's overall length and certainly the longest bill of any hummingbird. Although appearing as an overgrown appendage which may put it to a disadvantage, the Sword-billed Hummingbird is well adapted to feeding from long pendulous flower blooms. Its unusual appearance has also been instrumental in it gaining notoriety and thereby protection, by being listed as an attraction to many of the protected areas and national parks of Peru, Bolivia, Ecuador, and Colombia. It is a sedentary species ranging through the Andes from western Venezuela in the north to northern Bolivia where it prefers upper-montane forests, especially forest edges.

Not only does it feed by hovering below flowers, it will often perch or hang on flowers below to probe upward for nectar. It also hawks for insects, looking very ungainly as it darts about with its huge bill wide open.

The male has both upper and underparts a dark green, with a reddish tinge on the head, and black on the chin and throat. The underparts often appear iridescent and grayish on the lower belly. Both the forked tail and long wings are greenish-black. It has a small white spot behind the eye. Females are similar but duller with the tail less forked and pale-edged outer tail feathers. Her underparts differ in being grayish-buff with darker green spots.

Little is known of the breeding habits of the Sword-billed Hummingbird probably due to inaccessible nest sites high in the tree canopy.

Giant Hummingbird

Patagona gigas

7¾–8¾" (20–22cm)

Compared to the Bee Hummingbird, this is literally a giant and without doubt the largest of the hummingbird family.

Two races are recognized; *P. g. gigas* breeds in Chile and western Argentina and migrates across the Andes into northwest Argentina in the fall. The more northern race, *P. g. peruviana,* is found in the Andes from southwest Columbia through Ecuador, Peru, and Bolivia to the Atacama Desert in north Chile. Its preferred habitat is rather dry and open with shrubs, cacti, and scattered small trees, but in some places it frequents streamside vegetation and hedgerows close to habitation.

Males are recognized by a conspicuous white rump accentuated against dull olive-brown upperparts and cinnamon-colored underparts and sides of the neck. The upper tail coverts and feathers surrounding the rump have distinctive white edges. Females can be very similar to males but are generally duller with more spotted underparts. All have a substantial straight black bill and brownish-green forked tails.

This species can weigh up to 23 grams but the norm is around 19. Not only does it hover with a slower than normal hummingbird wingbeat, it frequently flies and glides in a swift-like manner. It is less likely to hover than most hummingbirds and often feeds while perched.

Its diet is primarily flower nectar but it also consumes numerous insects, which it hawks from a perch or snatches while hovering amongst a swarm. A favorite flower seems to be the agave, a tropical fleshy-leafed

plant that has very tall flowering stalks and from which sisal is obtained. This plant is thought to have been introduced in Ecuador and north Peru during the 16th century and is probably the reason for a northward expansion of the species range. Other common food sources are the flowers of several tall cacti as well as many different shrubs, providing a succession of nectar sources within its established territory.

Although very territorial and of an aggressive nature, it can often be seen feeding in small groups where food sources are particularly abundant.

Its breeding season depends on its location. In Peru it extends from September for six or seven months. In Chile it is later and shorter; from October to January. But in Ecuador it is later still; from December to March. The nest is made from moss and lichen bound together with spiders' webs and lined with hair, wool, or soft fine plant fibers. It is usually situated on a branch of a tree but occasionally on a cactus. Usually two eggs are laid taking just under two weeks to hatch.

Green-backed Firecrown

Sephanoides sephanoides

4¼" (10½cm)

The breeding range of this species is from Tierra del Fuego in Argentina and across and up into the foothills of the Andes of Chile and Argentina as far as the Atacama Desert. Birds from the south of the range move northward to winter mainly in central Argentina. It is quite common and can be found on the coast and into the foothills up to an elevation of around 6,500ft (2,000m). Not only does it like the wilder habitat of forest clearings and edges where it congregates in substantial numbers around flowering trees, but it also frequents urban parkland and yards. It takes mainly nectar from flowering trees, shrubs, and other plants supplemented occasionally with insects gleaned from foliage.

Both male and female have bronze-green upperparts, the male only having an iridescent yellow-red crown and forehead. The slightly forked tail and the wings are also bronze-green. The underparts are buffish-white densely scattered with iridescent green and brownish spots. The density of spots increases at the flanks giving a suffused green-bronze appearance. There is a small white spot to the rear of the eye and the short straight bill is black.

Breeding takes place during the latter quarter of the year but few details of breeding are available. Tiny cup-shaped nests of plant fibers and spiders' webs are attached to branches, often overhanging water and the clutch size is, again, two.

Juan Fernandez Firecrown

Sephanoides fernandenis

4¾" (12cm)

Also called the Fernandez Firecrown this species is highly endangered, with only a few hundred birds known to exist on Robinson Crusoe Island off the west coast of Chile. Its decline is probably due to habitat erosion due to man's incursion into the Juan Fernandez group of islands. Destruction of habitat due to tree-cutting as well as from the introduced goats and rabbits, together with the smothering effects on regenerating plants caused by introduced bramble are all thought to be causes for the species decline. Although seeming to prefer shaded and more secluded habitats of forest and dense pockets of woodland it is often found near human habitation and even within towns when attracted by flowering trees. Well adapted to the many species of plant found in the region, it is particularly attracted to the *Dendroseris littoralis*. It seeks out nectar from flowers of many plants but seldom in the bright sunshine and more often well away from the ground.

This is one of the few hummingbirds with striking sexual dimorphism. The male is easily recognized by his dark orange plumage, brown-gray wings and iridescent fiery orange-yellow crown. The short bill is black. The very different female has yellow-green upperparts becoming bluish on the rump. The crown is iridescent purple-blue; the tail is blue-green with the outer feathers having white inner webs and the underparts are white with spotted iridescent green over the throat and flanks.

No reliable breeding records are available.

Greenish Puffleg

Haplophaedia aureliae

3½–4" (9–10cm)

The three races of the Greenish Puffleg are all from separate areas of the Andes in the far northwest of South America. Although mainly sedentary, some are forced to move to lower altitudes during severe weather. The nominate race *H. a. aureliae* is found on the eastern side of the Andes from Colombia southward just into Ecuador. *H. a. caucensis* keeps to the central and western Andes of Colombia extending northward and into the far east of Panama, while *H. a. russata* is found in the eastern Andes of Ecuador.

All prefer the montane and sub-montane humid and wet forests where they feed on flowering trees and shrubs below the tree canopy. They also take insects which they glean from the foliage. They establish feeding territories which are vigorously defended driving off any other birds which dare to approach.

All three races are very similar in appearance having iridescent green upperparts tinged reddish with the top of the head and ear coverts a coppery-red. Underparts are dull green with very visible white leg puffs. The rump is reddish-bronze and the slightly notched tail Bluish-black. Between the races variations occur mainly on the breast and rump, although the Ecuadorian race has a slightly longer bill. Its underparts are dull brownish-green and upperparts a bright copper-red especially at the rump. *H. a. caucensis* has a patch of white on the lower belly and appears to have brighter green upperparts. All have straight black bills and a small white spot to the rear of the eye.

In the main breeding takes place between December and March when a nest site is chosen, well protected from inclement weather. The cup-shaped nest, often low down under heliconia leaves, is constructed mainly of mosses with a few plant fibers and spiders' webs. Two eggs are incubated by the female taking just over two weeks to hatch.

Booted Racquet-tail

Ocreatus underwoodii

6" (15cm)

Also called the Racquet-tail or Racquet-tailed Hummingbird, this is a very common species of montane forest throughout the Andes from northern Venezuela to Bolivia in the south. There are as many as eight races with some considerable differences between them. The nominate race, *O. u. underwoodii*, is found in the eastern Andes of Colombia and has both upperparts and underparts of iridescent green, although the forehead is more bronze-green. The male's deeply forked tail is green at the inner shorter feathers, becoming grayer towards the outers, which are substantially elongated at the tips into long black shafts with blue-black racquets at the ends. He has brownish-green ear coverts and a small white spot behind the eye. His legs and feet are almost hidden by large white leg puffs and his short straight bill is black. The female's upperparts are similar although the rump is occasionally finely spotted with buff. She has a short deeply forked green tail with bluish outer feathers tipped white. Her underparts are white medially becoming heavily spotted iridescent green at the flanks and her white leg puffs are somewhat smaller than the male's.

The male of *O. u. melanantherus* from Ecuador is very similar to the nominate race but has a black chin and bluish tips to the tail feathers. This female has more white and is less spotted on the underparts. The southern races, *O. u. addae*, *annae*, and *peruanus* all have rufous leg puffs. The more northern races, *O. u. polysticus* and *discifer* have bronzer upperparts, whereas *O. u. incommodus* from the west and central Andes of Colombia have an extensive patch of black over the chin and throat. All races are very adaptable to more open secondary forest as well as wet forest. They take nectar from flowering trees, shrubs, and bromeliads as well as hawking for insects.

There seems to be no particular breeding season, nests being found throughout the year. The small neat cup-shaped constructions are built with plant fibers and pieces of lichen on top of a thin branch. The female incubates two eggs for two and a half weeks and the young fledge about three weeks later.

Red-tailed Comet

Sappho sparganura

Male: 8" (20cm)

Female: 5" (13cm)

The nominate race of this beautiful, long-tailed hummingbird *Sappho s. sparganura* is spread through the arid Andes mountain slopes of northern and central Bolivia. The more orange colored southerly race *Sappho sparganura sappho* has a range that extends from southwestern Bolivia through western Argentina almost as far as the Callaqui and Villarica volcanoes. It has a local altitudinal migration, occurring at up to 13,000ft (4,000m) and moving down to lower elevations of around 5,000ft (1,500m) during the cold winter. Its habitat varies from more open semi-arid hillsides sparsely populated with small trees and bushes to dry deciduous forests. It feeds on a broad range of flower nectar as well as foraging and hawking for insects.

Males are recognized by their beautifully elongated and deeply forked and iridescent red or orange-red tail with the individual feathers broadly tipped blackish-purple. The back is red to reddish-purple and the head, throat, and a patch on the bend of the wing are all iridescent green. The underparts are green and the flight feathers dark green to black. The short, very slightly curved bill is black. Females also have a longish tail but much shorter than the males'. It is similarly colored but the barring shown by the black feather bands is much less distinct. The longer, outer tail feathers appear very pale on their outside edges. She has an iridescent green head and upperparts which become purplish at the rump. The underparts are buff heavily marked with green spots particularly at the throat.

This species prefers to nest on cliff faces and below overhanging rocks. The nest, a substantial, cup-shaped construction of moss, hair, and lichens is usually established on a ledge or fixed to exposed roots. Two eggs are laid and incubated by the female for nearly three weeks. The chicks fledge a little longer than three weeks later.

Blue-tufted Starthroat

Heliomaster furcifer

5" (13cm)

This species occurs particularly in the lowlands of the area extending from central and eastern Bolivia taking in southern Matto Grosso to Goias and Rio Grande du Sul in Brazil, Paraguay, western Uraguay, and northern Argentina. It prefers a grassland habitat often associated with trees and forest edges. Its main diet consists of nectar from a wide variety of flowering plants including trees, shrubs, cacti, herbs, and bromeliads. Aerial insects are also hawked from a prominent perch and other insects and spiders taken by foraging through foliage.

The male's upperparts are iridescent bronze-green with the forehead, crown, nape, and upper mantle bright blue-green. The sharp forked tail is green, dark above and with a blue sheen below. The gorget is iridescent dark-blue with a patch of brilliant violet in the center of the throat and the feathers at the sides of the neck extended backward almost to the nape. The underparts are also very dark iridescent blue, becoming green toward the vent. The long, slightly decurved bill is black. The female is more mundanely colored, having brownish-green upperparts with a coppery-red crown and nape. The underparts are generally gray with a patch of grayish-white on the lower belly and a green tinge at the flanks. Her tail shows dark-green above becoming darker towards the tip and from below it is brilliant blue-green with white tips on the outer feathers. After breeding the male goes into an eclipse plumage, losing his dark blue coloration and appearing very similar to the female.

The breeding season is from late November to March. The nest site often ten to 20 feet (three to six meters) off the ground, is on top of a branch. A cup-shaped nest is constructed of fine plant fibers interwoven with a few spiders' webs and decorated externally with pieces of lichen. The female incubates the two eggs for a little over two weeks and the young fledge three to four weeks later.

Oasis Hummingbird

Rhodopis vesper

5–5½" (13–13½cm)

This mainly sedentary species has three races distributed along the western slopes and coastal hills bordering the Andes through Peru to the Atacama Desert in northern Chile. The nominate race, *R. v. vesper*, is found from northwest Peru southward and just into northern Chile. The race *R. v. atacamensis* occurs within the Atacama Desert, whereas *R. v. koepckeae* is restricted to a small area in the far northwest of Peru. It occurs from the arid mountainous zones below around 10,000ft (3,000m) right down into hilly and lowland coastal areas where it is most common. It prefers to feed from nectar bearing flowers of trees, shrubs, and cacti and can therefore be found in oases as its name implies but it is also frequently seen close to human habitation in parks and yards. Its diet is also supplemented by insects and spiders caught by gleaning or hawking.

Males have olive-green upperparts with a bright sheen becoming chestnut at the rump and on the upper tail coverts. The deeply forked tail is dark brown, tinged purple with the central feathers being lighter. The underparts are whitish becoming greenish at the flanks. The throat and neck are a bright iridescent violet with turquoise blue patches below the ear coverts and there is a white eyebrow. The long and slightly curved bill is black. Females have similar olive-green upperparts but lack the bright throat and neck coloration having dirty-white underparts. The white eyebrow is also less pronounced. She has a shorter and only slightly forked tail which is mainly olive-green, but black toward the ends of the outer feathers with white tips. It is pale gray below.

Breeding occurs from September to November with nests being constructed in low fruit trees amongst the outer branches. Cup-shaped suspended nests of plant fibers, hair, lichen, and pieces of dry leaf are held together with spiders' webs. Two eggs are incubated by the female for a little over two weeks and the young fledge around three and a half weeks later.

Magenta-throated Woodstar

Calliphlox bryantae

3½" (9cm)

This small hummingbird enjoys the southern mountain slopes of an area extending from northern Costa Rica to Western Panama. Its favorite habitat seems to be close to forest edges and in clearings, it likes open areas of grassland and pasture with a scattering of shrubs and trees in particular and, at times, large numbers can congregate in such places. It depends upon nectar from flowering shrubs, trees, and plants often very close to the ground and it also gleans insects and spiders from foliage as well as hawking flies from a prominent perch. The typical feeding posture especially of the male is to raise the forked tail high while keeping it closed.

As its name implies, the throat, or gorget, of at least the male is a brilliant iridescent magenta-purple. Below his gorget is a broad white band that runs right around the upper-breast almost to the nape. Around the center of the breast is a glittering green band that blends into a thin band of rufous which gives way to a whitish vent. The upperparts are bronze-green and there is a white spot behind the eye. The long and deeply forked tail is blackish-green with the short inner feathers tipped black. The inner webs of the outer feathers are reddish-brown. The black bill is short and straight. The female has bronze-green upperparts but lacks the magenta gorget of the male. She has mainly whitish underparts which are green and rufous at the flanks. The throat is buffish at the chin and white below, bordered by a pale rufous band leading up to grayish ear coverts. She has a shorter forked tail shaped as two round lobes. The inner feathers are bronze with a black sub-terminal band and the outer feathers are rufous also with a black sub-terminal band but the tips are pale rufous.

Breeding is thought to take place between November and April but no reliable breeding data is currently available.

Ruby-throated Hummingbird

Archilochus colubris

3½" (9cm)

The Ruby-throated Hummingbird is the most widespread hummingbird in the United States and Canada, being found throughout central and eastern US from the Gulf coast northward into a band across southern Canada from Nova Scotia to central Alberta. It migrates there for the breeding season from its wintering grounds in central Mexico southward into western Panama although some remain in southern Florida. The migration path taken by most of these birds follows a route around the Gulf of Mexico although records show that some attempt the journey across the Gulf, often being stranded by bad weather on the islands to the south of Florida. Wintering habitat is primarily dry lowland forests and scrub but breeding takes place more in mixed woodland habitat including low-lying secondary forests. It is also frequently observed in more open parkland as well as domestic yards. It feeds from a wide variety of flowering plants and shrubs, being particularly attracted to those which are red in color. A large amount of insects and spiders are also consumed, especially during migration when flowering plants may not always be available. Although insects are gleaned from foliage, this species is very adept at flycatching.

The gorget of the male is an iridescent ruby red bordered above by a black stripe passing from the lores and below the eye and through the ear coverts. Below is a white band blending into a grayish belly with greenish flanks. From the forehead to the rump the upperparts are an iridescent green down to the central feathers of the forked tail. The outer tail feathers are brownish-gray. It has a small white spot behind the eye and a short, straight, dark-colored bill. The female lacks the ruby throat having all white underparts speckled gray-green at the throat and washed gray at the flanks.

The breeding season lasts from April to late July, the male arriving in his breeding territory a few days prior to the females. Cup-shaped nests are constructed, almost entirely by the female, on top of horizontal branches from plant fibers and lichens bound together with spiders' webs and decorated externally with pieces of lichen. Two eggs are incubated by the female for just over two weeks, the young fledging after a further two to three weeks.

Right: **Female.**

Below: **Male.**

Black-chinned Hummingbird

Archilochus alexandri

4" (10cm)

This migratory species breeds from southwest Canada through the western United States, south as far as Baja California and northern Mexico, and eastward as far as the Gulf of Mexico. It winters in western and southern Mexico where a number are also thought to be resident. Breeding can start as early as March in the south of its range but is some two to three months later further north. A large proportion of the migrants have accomplished their long journey south by September.

During the breeding season they occupy woodland and scrub often in arid regions and also in desert scrubland with adjacent rivers, seldom going above 6,500ft (2,000m).

They rely on nectar from a succession of flowering plants as well as small flies, which are hawked in the air.

The male's plumage is a medium iridescent green over the upperparts with white underparts becoming green at the flanks. The wings and forked tail are a dark green with the outer tail feathers appearing lighter. His chin is black, extending in a triangle back beyond the eye taking in the ear coverts. This area of black becomes iridescent violet along its bottom edge. There is a small white spot behind the eye. The longish bill is dark brown-black. Females are very similar but have the chin, ear coverts, and throat whitish with buff spots on the throat. Her tail is more rounded having white tips to the outer three feathers. She is almost impossible to distinguish from the female Ruby-throated Hummingbird (*Archilochus colubris*).

A cup-shaped nest is constructed from a mixture of lichens, pieces of leaf and bark, and plant down held together with spiders' webs usually sited on the top of a branch some ten feet (three meters) above ground and overhanging running water. In some areas it is noted that a large number of yellow plant "hairs" are worked into the nest construction. The female usually incubates her two eggs for just over a fortnight, fledging taking up to three weeks.

Right: **Male.**

Below: **Female.**

Anna's Hummingbird

Calypte anna

4–4½" (10–11cm)

This species is confined mainly to the western United States and Canada with movements occurring southward down into Mexico and Baja, California. In recent years it has extended its winter range southeastward into the central area of northern Mexico and is occasionally found further east. Its breeding range is from northwest Mexico through western USA, taking in a large area of southern Arizona, to southwest Canada.

It occurs up to 6,000ft (1,800m) in a wide variety of habitats from coastal scrub, through river valleys, to woodland—especially oaks and evergreens—and often close to human habitation in towns and cities.

Nectar from flowering plants provides a major food source but it also consumes quantities of small flies and spiders which it hawks or gleans from foliage.

The upperparts of the male are a bright yellow-green and the underparts appear a dirty grayish-green. His head is masked with iridescent red coloring reaching down to the extended feathers of the gorget. The tail is bronze-green. The shortish bill is black. Females lack the bright red head coloration being grayish instead often with pink spots on the throat and a small white spot behind the eye. Her outer-tail feathers have white tips.

In favorable weather conditions, breeding commences as early as November and extends through to May or even July at higher altitudes. The nest site is usually on a horizontal branch or twig anywhere from six feet (two meters) above ground to the tops of tall trees. Plant fibers, animal hair, and feathers are bound together with spiders' webs to form a cup-shaped nest and then decorated externally with small pieces of lichen, leaves, and bark. The female incubates two eggs from two to two and a half weeks. Another two and a half to three and a half weeks are taken for the young to fledge.

Costa's Hummingbird

Calypte costae

3–3½" (7½–8½cm)

Costa's Hummingbird is a partial migrant most birds moving south to spend their winter in the south and west of Mexico, migrating north into the western United States to breed. It reaches to the north as far as southwest Utah and southern Nevada and into central California to breed, but after breeding some birds disperse to reach as far north as southern Canada and to Texas in the east. Its breeding area is mainly north of central Sonora.

This is a lowland species, seldom venturing higher than the foothills. During the breeding season, they are found in open dry country from areas of coastal scrub through desert, semi-desert, and into scrubby areas of the foothills. They naturally seek out areas where flowering shrubs are abundant and often a variety of trees are present. Males set up their territories in very open areas and females are only present there for the duration of the breeding period. After breeding females and young move away into more lush vegetation and are found particularly in lowland meadows, yards, and among fruit trees.

Besides being a nectar feeder, Costa's Hummingbird consumes large quantities of insects and spiders. It will glean amongst shrubs and plant foliage and also hawk for aerial insects as they swarm.

The very attractive plumage of the male is accentuated by its brilliant colored mask. Both the crown and gorget of elongated plumes are a dark iridescent violet standing out from the dull bronze-green upperparts. The upper breast is white, extending beneath the gorget around the cheek to beyond the eye. There is a band of greenish-bronze across the center of the breast, which merges into a pale gray belly and vent. The short rounded tail is a bronze-green, the central feathers being tipped black and the three outers being grayish tipped white with a narrow black sub-terminal band. Females are much duller but with upperparts similar to males. They lack the male's violet crown and gorget and have only a brownish-green crown and a dirty white chin and throat. Occasionally there are a few purple markings on the throat. It has a short and straight blackish bill.

Breeding starts as early as February when the males set up their territories. The nest site can be up to ten feet (three meters) above ground in the thick outer foliage of a shrub or tree but occasionally a more open site such as a cactus is chosen. A cup-shaped nest is constructed from plant fibers and spiders' webs decorated on the outside with small pieces of lichen, dry leaf, grass, and bark. Plant down and tiny feathers are often used as lining. The female incubates two eggs for a little over two weeks and the young take about three weeks to fledge.

Above right: **Male.**

Right: **Female.**

Calliope Hummingbird

Stellula calliope

2¾–3" (7–7½cm)

This species is recognized as North America's smallest bird. Many migrate 2,800 miles (45,00km) from their wintering grounds in the southwest part of central Mexico to breed as far north as southwest Canada. Others choose to stop off in the cool montane regions of the Sierra Nevada stretching from Washington to southern California and also eastward to the Rocky Mountains. Here they search out as suitable breeding territory, areas of new growth after logging or forest fires where shrubs and low trees proliferate. Their wintering habitat is very similar, often associated with shrubby growth following fires, but they are also found in scrub bordering agricultural and ranching land as well as open pine-oak forest. During the breeding season they depend in particular on a succession of a wide range of colorful tubular shaped flowers amongst which they can forage for nectar. They also hawk amongst hordes of tiny flying insects. The situation is slightly different in the winter habitat where competition with other species of hummingbird and warblers forces them to seek out plant sources in lesser demand.

The male is recognized by his unusual gorget—an array of iridescent purple-magenta elongated feathers emanating under the chin and spreading outward as radial lines. The upperparts are metallic bronze-green and underparts whitish with a green tinge at the flanks.

The tips of the dark green wing primaries extend past the tip of the tail as the bird is perched. The short tail is greenish-black and the short, straight bill is black. The female is similar to the male but lacks the gorget and has a whitish throat spotted with brown markings. She also has buffish underparts. Her tail feathers are black with the three outers tipped with white spots.

Nesting occurs during May to July when a cup-shaped nest is constructed amongst foliage, often in a conifer, where it will be protected above from adverse weather. Very fine plant fibers are held together with spiders' webs and covered on the outside by a collection of lichens and bits of bark and moss. The inside is lined with plant down. The female incubates her two eggs for just over two weeks and the young fledge after a further three.

Scintillant Hummingbird

Selasphorus scintilla

2¾" (7cm)

Found only in a confined area of the mountains of Costa Rica and western Panama, and then mainly on the southern slopes, this small hummingbird is more a bird of open countryside. It is found particularly in pastureland scattered with shrubby growth and hedgerows and often approaches human habitation, coming into yards and agricultural land. Shrubby growth within plantations and along forest edges are also exploited. Nectar is taken from a wide variety of small flowers but mainly from low-growing plants and shrubs. Insects and spiders are gleaned from foliage, especially along hedgerows and hawking for insects is often undertaken from a prominent perch.

The male has all bronze-green upperparts, contrasting with a mainly rufous tail. The shafts of inner tail feathers are bordered with a black longitudinal band and the outer three tail feathers have a black sub-terminal band. He has an orange-red gorget with extended feathers at the rear and a small white spot behind the eye. Below the gorget and along the top of the breast is a white band that blends into a rufous-buff with greenish markings towards the flanks leaving a whitish patch down the center of the belly. Both the vent and undertail coverts are a pale rufous color. The short, straight bill is black. The female is similar but less bright and missing the red gorget. She has a buff-colored throat spotted with dark gray, becoming almost black at the ear coverts. Her tail also differs in having a broader sub-terminal black band and a greenish tinge to the inner feathers.

Breeding is confined mainly to the wet season through from September to February when a suitable site is chosen; usually on an outside branch of a shrub but occasionally amongst tall grasses. The small and delicate nest is composed of very fine plant fibers and thistledown with pieces of moss, lichen, and treefern bound together with spiders' webs and occasionally lined with tiny soft feathers. The outside may be covered with pieces of moss and lichen. The egg clutch size is usually two but no other breeding details have been confirmed.

Broad-tailed Hummingbird

Selasphorus platycercus

4" (10cm)

Above: **Male.**

Above right: **Female.**

The breeding range of this mainly migrant species covers an area from highland Guatemala northward through the highlands of Mexico and into the USA. Here it is spread through southwest Texas and Arizona and up into eastern California, Nevada, Utah, southern Idaho, and Wyoming. The migrants, mainly from the north of the range, winter in the south from Mexico to Guatemala. It prefers woodland and meadows between 5,000ft (1,500m) and 8,000ft (2,500m) often being found close to rivers and streams. Its main diet is nectar from flowering ground-hugging shrubs and herbs but it does glean foliage for spiders and insects as well as hawking flies in the air.

The upperparts of the male are a dark olive-green with a bronze tinge to the central tail feathers. The remaining tail feathers are blackish-purple tinged red on the outer webs. The gorget is iridescent bright red below which is a white breast band that stretches in a narrow stripe upward and behind the dark olive ear coverts. The lower breast is whitish becoming green at the flanks. His short, straight bill is black. The female is more yellow-green above and has green central tail feathers. The remaining tail feathers are rufous right at the base becoming green toward a black sub-terminal band and finally tipped

white. She has whitish underparts, pale rufous at the flanks and vent, and spotted rufous-gray on the throat.

Breeding takes place between April and July when a little cup-shaped nest, mainly of very fine plant fibers, is constructed on a branch frequently overhanging water. Small pieces of lichen, bark, twig, and leaves are used to decorate and disguise the external appearance. The female incubates a clutch of two eggs for two and a half weeks. The chicks take three to four weeks to fledge.

Rufous Hummingbird

Selasphorus rufus

3½" (8½cm)

This migratory species spends its winter mainly in the highlands of Mexico but it is regularly seen all along the USA's Gulf coast and southern Texas. It migrates northwards early in the year arriving in Oregon in late February and spreading way northward as flowering plants become available. Eventually it spreads out throughout its breeding range covering northwest USA and southwest Canada as far north as southeastern Alaska and eastward to western Alberta. It obviously prefers the cool climates with a wide variety of flowering plants, but is known to take tree sap from holes made by woodpeckers when flowers are less numerous. Flowering trees are exploited, as are plants such as the opuntias and agaves, and spiders and insects taken when gleaning through foliage. Within its breeding range it seems to prefer clearings and forest edges particularly secondary growth and thorn forest.

As would be expected, the male is of outstanding rufous plumage, in particularly its upperparts. The gorget is iridescent scarlet-red changing to bright green as the lighting changes. Below this is a white upper-chest band which becomes rufous on the belly. The forehead, crown, and a patch at the bend of the wing are bronze-green and the rounded tail rufous tipped black. The female has predominantly bronze-green upperparts down to the central tail feathers. The outer tail feathers are rufous at the base, having green then black sub-terminal bands before being tipped white. Her underparts are dirty white with a whitish neck and throat. The throat is often covered with iridescent bronze spots.

Nesting sites are variable but usually on a branch of a shrub or tree, the cup-shaped nest being constructed from mixed plant fibers bound together with spiders' webs and decorated externally with small pieces of lichen, moss, bark, and leaf. The female incubates two eggs for two and a half weeks, the young fledging about three weeks later.

Right: **Male.**

Below: **Female.**

Allen's Hummingbird

Selasphorus sasin

3¾" (9½cm)

Two races of this species exist; the sedentary *S. s. sedentarius* being found on the islands off southern California, while the nominate and migratory race (*S. s. sasin*) winters in southern central Mexico and breeds from southern California northward into the borders of Oregon. Both races seem to favor a more open and scrubby habitat with a preference for more humid conditions found in canyons and beside streams during the breeding season. After breeding, they will disperse and be found along forest edges and in more open coniferous and deciduous woodland as well as grassland with plenty of shrubby growth. They are nectar feeders with a particular attraction for flowering trees and shrubs and they will also hawk for aerial insects.

As for plumage, this species is frequently confused with the Rufous Hummingbird (*Selasphorus rufus*) where their ranges overlap in southern California. Males can be distinguished by their iridescent all-green back and nape, which are rufous on the Rufous Hummingbird. However, females and immature birds are virtually indistinguishable. Besides having a green back, the male's forehead and crown are also iridescent green. The rump and upper tail coverts are rufous leading into tail feathers, which are rufous at the base and tipped black. Black edges show on the outer vanes of the outer two tail feathers. The gorget is a brilliant orange-red, below which is a band of white stretching across the breast and narrowing towards the nape. The rest of the underparts are rufous and the shortish black bill is almost straight. There is a small white spot behind the eye and a broad rufous eyestripe passing from the lores above and below the eye, between crown and gorget, to the nape. Females and immature individuals have predominantly bronze-green upperparts down to and including the central tail feathers. The outer tail feathers are rufous at the base, having green then black sub-terminal bands before being tipped white. Her underparts are dirty white becoming rufous at the flanks and she has a whitish neck and throat. The throat is often covered with iridescent bronze spots becoming denser over the ear coverts.

The breeding season is throughout the year for the island race (*S. s. sedentarius*) but confined to spring and early summer for migrants (*s. s. sasin*). Tree sites are usually chose for nesting and the nest is built from plant fibers and down, incorporating moss, hair, and lichen, with liberal amounts of spiders' webs to hold it together. The female, who has constructed the nest also incubates the eggs alone for two to three weeks. She also feeds the young during the fledging period of around three and a half weeks. Often two broods are attempted.

Right: **Male.**

Below: **Female.**

A Checklist of Hummingbirds of the World

Phaethornithinae

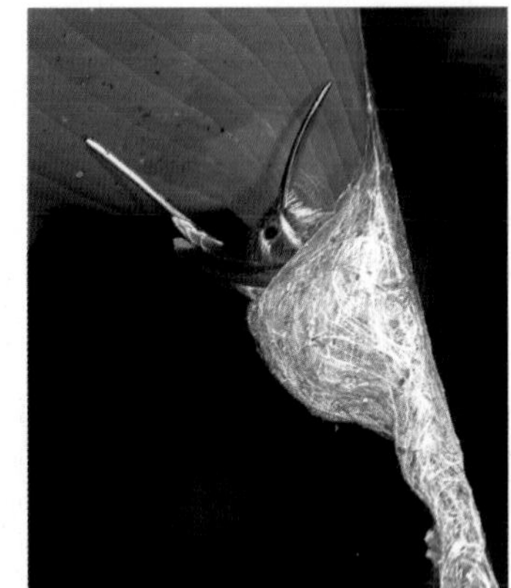

Saw-billed Hermit	*Ramphodon naevis*
White-tipped Sicklebill	*Eutoxeres aquila*
Buff-tailed Sicklebill	*Eutoxeres condamini*
Hook-Billed Hermit	*Glaucis dohrnii*
Hairy Hermit	*Glaucis hirsuta*
Bronzy Hermit	*Glaucis aenea*
Band-tailed Barbthroat	*Threnetes ruckeri*
Pale-tailed Barbthroat	*Threnetes niger*
Broad-tipped Hermit	*Anopetia gounellei*
White-whiskered Hermit	*Phaethornis yaruqui*
Green Hermit	*Phaethornis guy*
White-bearded Hermit (left)	*Phaethornis hispidus*
Western long-tailed Hermit	*Phaethornis longirostris*
Eastern long-tailed Hermit	*Phaethornis superciliosus*
Great-billed Hermit	*Phaethornis malaris*
Tawny-bellied Hermit	*Phaethornis syrmatophorus*
Koepcke's Hermit	*Phaethornis koepckeae*
Needle-billed Hermit	*Phaethornis philippii*
Straight-billed Hermit	*Phaethornis bourcieri*
Pale-bellied Hermit	*Phaethornis anthophilus*
Scale-throated Hermit	*Phaethornis eurynome*
Planalto Hermit	*Phaethornis pretrei*
Sooty-capped Hermit	*Phaethornis augusti*
Buff-bellied Hermit	*Phaethornis subochraceus*
Dusky-throated hermit	*Phaethornis squalidus*
Streak-throated Hermit	*Phaethornis rupurumii*
Little Hermit	*Phaethornis longuemareus*
Minute Hermit	*Phaethornis idaliae*
Cinnamon-throated Hermit	*Phaethornis nattereri*
Reddish Hermit	*Phaethornis ruber*
White-browed Hermit	*Phaethornis stuarti*
Black-throated Hermit	*Phaethornis atrimentalis*
Stripe-throated Hermit	*Phaethornis striigularis*
Grey-chinned Hermit	*Phaethornis griseogularis*

Trochilinae

Tooth-billed Hummingbird	*Androdon aequatorialis*
Green-fronted Lancebill	*Doryfera ludovicae*
Blue-fronted Lancebill	*Doryfera johannae*
Scaly-breasted Hummingbird	*Campylopterus cuvierii*
Wedge-tailed Sabrewing	*Campylopterus curvipennis*
Grey-breasted Sabrewing	*Campylopterus largipennis*
Rufous Sabrewing	*Campylopterus rufus*
Rufous-breasted Sabrewing	*Campylopterus hyperythrus*
Violet Sabrewing	*Campylopterus hemileucurus*
White-tailed Sabrewing	*Campylopterus ensipennis*

Right: **Anna's Hummingbird.**

Lazuline Sabrewing	*Campylopterus falcatus*
Santa Marta Sabrewing	*Campylopterus phainopeplus*
Napo Sabrewing	*Campylopterus villaviscensio*
Buff-reasted Sabrewing	*Campylopterus duidae*
Sombre Hummingbird	*Campylopterus cirrochloris*
Swallow-tailed Hummingbird	*Campylopterus macrourus*
White-necked Jacobin	*Florisuga mellivora*
Black Jacobin	*Florisuga fusca*
Brown Violet-ear	*Colibri delphinae*
Green Violet-ear	*Colibri thalassinus*
Sparkling Violet-ear	*Colibri coruscans*
White-vented Violet-ear	*Colibri serrirostris*
Green-throated Mango	*Anthracothorax viridigula*
Green-breasted Mango	*Anthracothorax prevostii*
Black-throated Mango	*Anthracothorax nigricollis*
Veragues Mango	*Anthracothorax veraguensis*
Antillean Mango	*Anthracothorax dominicus*
Green Mango (left)	*Anthracothorax viridis*
Jamaican Mango	*Anthracothorax mango*
Fiery-throated Awlbill	*Anthracothorax recurvirostris*
Crimson Topaz	*Topaza pella*
Purple-throated Carib	*Eulampis jugularis*
Green-throated Carib	*Eulampis holosericeus*
Ruby Topaz	*Chrysolampis mosquitus*
Antillean Crested Hummingbird	*Orthorhynchus cristatus*
Violet-headed Hummingbird	*Klais guimeti*
Plovercrest	*Stephanoxis lalandi*
Emerald-chinned Hummingbird	*Abeillia abeillei*
Tufted Coquette	*Lophornis ornatus*
Dot-eared Coquette	*Lophornis gouldii*
Frilled Coquette	*Lophornis magnificus*
Short-crested Coquette	*Lophornis brachylophus*
Rufous-crested Coquette	*Lophornis delattrei*
Spangled Coquette	*Lophornis stictolophus*
Festive Coquette	*Lophornis chalybeus*
Peacock Coquette	*Lophornis pavoninus*
Black-crested Coquette	*Lophornis helenae*
White-crested Coquette	*Lophornis adorabilis*
Wire-crested Thorntail	*Discosura popelairii*
Black-bellied Thorntail	*Discosura langsdorfi*
Coppery Thorntail	*Discosura letitiae*
Green Thorntail	*Discosura conversii*
Racquet-tailed Coquette	*Discosura longicauda*
Red-billed Streamertail	*Trochilus polytmus*
Black-billed Streamertail	*Trochilus scitulus*
Blue-chinned Sapphire	*Chlorostilbon notatus*
Blue-tailed Emerald	*Chlorostilbon mellisugus*
Chiribiquete Emerald	*Chlorostilbon olivaresi*
Glittering-bellied Emerald	*Chlorostilbon aureoventris*
Cuban Emerald (left)	*Chlorostilbon ricordii*
Hispaniolan Emerald	*Chlorostilbon swainsonii*

Puerto Rican Emerald	*Chlorostilbon maugaeus*
Coppery Emerald	*Chlorostilbon russatus*
Narrow-tailed Emerald	*Chlorostilbon stenurus*
Green-tailed Emerald	*Chlorostilbon alice*
Short-tailed Emerald	*Chlorostilbon poortmani*
Fiery-throated Hummingbird	*Panterpe insignis*
White-tailed Emerald	*Elvira chionura*
Coppery-headed Emerald	*Elvira cupreiceps*
Oaxaca Hummingbird	*Eupherusa cyanophrys*
White-tailed Hummingbird	*Eupherusa poliocerca*
Stripe-tailed Hummingbird	*Eupherusa eximia*
Black-bellied Hummingbird	*Eupherusa nigriventris*
Pirre Hummingbird	*Goethalsia bella*
VioletT-capped Hummingbird	*Goldmania violiceps*
Dusky Hummingbird	*Cynanthus sordidus*
Broad-billed Hummingbird (right)	*Cynanthus latirostris*
Blue-headed Hummingbird	*Cyanophaia bicolor*
Mexican Woodnymph	*Thalurania ridgwayi*
Purple-crowned Woodnymph	*Thalurania columbica*
Green-crowned Woodnymph	*Thalurania fannyi*
Fork-tailed Woodnymph	*Thalurania furcata*
Long-tailed Woodnymph	*Thalurania watertonii*
Violet-capped Woodnymph	*Thalurania glaucopis*
Violet-bellied Hummingbird	*Damophila julie*
Sapphire-throated Hummingbird	*Lepidopyga coeruleogularis*
Sapphire-bellied Hummingbird	*Lepidopyga lilliae*
Shining Green Hummingbird	*Lepidopyga goudoti*
Blue-throated Goldentail	*Hylocharis eliciae*
Rufous-throated Sapphire	*Hylocharis sapphirina*
White-chinned Sapphire	*Hylocharis cyanus*
Gilded Hummingbird	*Hylocharis chrysura*
Blue-headed Sapphire	*Hylocharis grayi*
Golden-tailed Sapphire	*Chrysuronia oenone*
White-throated Hummingbird	*Leucochloris albicollis*
White-tailed Goldenthroat	*Polytmus guainumbi*
Tepui Goldenthroat	*Polytmus milleri*
Green-tailed Goldenthroat	*Polytmus theresiae*
Buffy Hummingbird	*Leucippus fallax*
Tumbes Hummingbird	*Leucippus baeri*
Spot-throated Hummingbird	*Leucippus taczanowskii*
Olive-spotted Hummingbird	*Leucippus chlorocercus*
White-bellied Hummingbird	*Leucippus chionogaster*
Green & White Hummingbird	*Leucippus viridicauda*
Many-spotted Hummingbird	*Leucippus hypostictus*
Rufous-tailed Hummingbird (right)	*Amazilia tzacatl*
Chestnut-bellied Hummingbird	*Amazilia castaneiventris*
Amazalia Hummingbird	*Amazilia amazalia*
Loja Hummingbird	*Amazilia alticola*
Buff-bellied Hummingbird	*Amazilia yucatanensis*
Cinnamon Hummingbird	*Amazilia rutila*
Plain-bellied Emerald	*Agyrtria leucogaster*

Versicolored Emerald	*Agyrtria versicolor*
Blue-Green Emerald	*Agyrtria rondoniae*
White-chested Emerald	*Agyrtria brevirostris*
Andean Emerald	*Agyrtria franciae*
White-bellied Emerald	*Agyrtria candida*
Azure-crowned Hummingbird	*Agyrtria cyanocephala*
Violet-crowned Hummingbird	*Agyrtria violiceps*
Green-fronted Hummingbird	*Agyrtria viridifrons*
Glittering-throated Emerald	*Polyerata fimbriata*
Sapphire-spangeled Emerald	*Polyerata lactea*
Blue-chested Hummingbird	*Polyerata amabilis*
Purple-chested Hummingbird	*Polyerata rosenbergi*
Mangrove Hummingbird	*Polyerata boucardi*
Honduran Emerald	*Polyerata luciae*
Steely-vented Hummingbird	*Saucerottia saucerrottei*
Indigo-capped Hummingbird	*Saucerottia cyanifrons*
Snowy-breasted Hummingbird	*Saucerottia edward*
Blue-tailed Hummingbird	*Saucerottia cyanura*
Berylline Hummingbird	*Saucerottia beryllina*
Green-bellied Hummingbird	*Saucerottia viridigaster*
Copper-tailed Hummingbird	*Saucerottia cupreicauda*
Copper-rumped Hummingbird	*Saucerottia tobaci*
Snowcap (left)	*Microchera albocoronata*
Blossomcrown	*Anthocephala floriceps*
White-veined Plumeleteer	*Chalybura buffonii*
Bronze-tailed Plumeleteer	*Chalybura urochrysia*
Blue-throated Hummingbird	*Lampornis clemenciae*
Amethyst-throated Hummingbird	*Lampornis amethystinus*
Green-throated Mountain-Gem	*Lampornis viridipallens*
Green-breasted mountain-gem	*Lampornis sybillae*
White-bellied Mountain-Gem	*Lampornis hemileucus*
Variable Mountain-gem	*Lampornis castaneoventris*
Xantuss Hummingbird	*Basilinna xantusii*
White-eared Hummingbird (left)	*Basilinna leucotis*
Garnet-throated Hummingbird	*Lamprolaima rhami*
Speckled Hummingbird	*Adelomyia melanogenys*
Ecuadorian Piedtail	*Phlogophilus hemileucurus*
Peruvian Piedtail	*Phlogophilus harterti*
Brazilian Ruby	*Clytolaema rubricauda*
Gould's Jewelfront	*Heliodoxa aurescens*
Fawn-breasted Brilliant	*Heliodoxa rubinoides*
Violet-fronted Brilliant	*Heliodoxa leadbeateri*
Velvet-browed Brilliant	*Heliodoxa xanthogonys*
Black-throated Brilliant	*Heliodoxa schreibersii*
Pink-throated Brilliant	*Heliodoxa gularis*
Rufous-webbed Brilliant	*Heliodoxa branickii*
Empress Brilliant	*Heliodoxa imperatrix*
Green-fronted Brilliant	*Heliodoxa jacula*
Magnificent Hummingbird	*Eugenes fulgens*
Scissor-tailed Hummingbird	*Hylonympha macrocerca*
Violet-chested Hummingbird	*Sternclyta cyanopectus*

White-tailed Hillstar	*Urochroa bougueri*
Buff-tailed Coronet	*Boissonneaua flavescens*
Chestnut-breasted Coronet	*Boissonneaua matthewsii*
Velvet-Purple Coronet	*Boissonneaua jardini*
Shining Sunbeam	*Aglaeactis cupripennis*
White-tufted Sunbeam	*Aglaeactis castelnaudii*
Purple-backed Sunbeam	*Aglaeactis aliciae*
Black-hooded Sunbeam	*Aglaeactis pamela*
Andean Hillstar (right)	*Oreotrochilus estella*
Ecuadorian Hillstar	*Oreotrochilus chimborazo*
Green-headed Hillstar	*Oreotrochilus stolzmanni*
White-sided Hillstar	*Oreotrochilus leucopleurus*
Black-breasted Hillstar	*Oreotrochilus melanogaster*
Wedge-tailed Hillstar	*Oreotrochilus adela*
Mountain Velvetbreast	*Lafresnaya lafresnayi*
Bronzy Inca	*Coeligena coeligena*
Brown Inca	*Coeligena wilsoni*
Black Inca	*Coeligena prunellei*
Collared Inca	*Coeligena torquata*
Gould's Inca	*Coeligena inca*
White-tailed Starfrontlet	*Coeligena phalerata*
Golden Starfrontlet	*Coeligena eos*
Golden-bellied Starfrontlet	*Coeligena bonapartei*
Blue-throated Starfrontlet	*Coeligena helianthea*
Buff-winged Starfrontlet	*Coeligena lutetiae*
Violet-throated Starfrontlet	*Coeligena violifer*
Rainbow Starfrontlet	*Coeligena iris*
Sword-billed Hummingbird	*Ensifera ensifera*
Great Sapphirewing	*Pterophanes cyanopterus*
Giant Hummingbird (right)	*Patagona gigas*
Green-backed Firecrown	*Sephanoides sephanoides*
Juan Fernandez Firecrown	*Sephanoides fernandensis*
Orange-throated Sunangel	*Heliangelus mavors*
Longuemare's Sunangel	*Heliangelus clarissae*
Amethyst-throated Sunangel	*Heliangelus amethysticollis*
Gorgeted Sunangel	*Heliangelus strophianus*
Tourmaline Sunangel	*Heliangelus exortis*
Little Sunangel	*Heliangelus micraster*
Purple-throated Sunangel	*Heliangelus viola*
Royal Sunangel	*Heliangelus regalis*
Black-breasted Puffleg	*Eriocnemis nigrivestris*
Glowing Puffleg	*Eriocnemis vestitus*
Black-thighed Puffleg	*Eriocnemis derbyi*
Turquoise-throated Puffleg	*Eriocnemis godini*
Coppery-bellied Puffleg	*Eriocnemis cupreoventris*
Sapphire-vented Puffleg	*Eriocnemis luciani*
Coppery-naped Puffleg	*Eriocnemis sapphiropygia*
Golden-breasted Puffleg	*Eriocnemis mosquera*
Blue-capped Puffleg	*Eriocnemis glaucopoides*
Colorful Puffleg	*Eriocnemis mirabilis*
Emerald-bellied Puffleg	*Eriocnemis alinae*

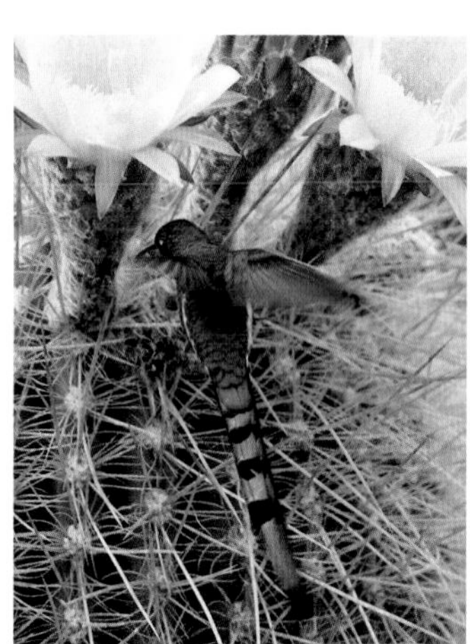

Greenish Puffleg (right)	*Haplophaedia aureliae*
Buff-thighed Puffleg	*Haplophaedia assimilis*
Hoary Puffleg	*Haplophaedia lugens*
Purple-bibbed Whitetip	*Urosticte benjamini*
Rufous-vented Whitetip	*Urosticte ruficrissa*
Booted Racquet-tail	*Ocreatus underwoodii*
Black-tailed Trainbearer	*Lesbia victoriae*
Green-tailed Trainbearer	*Lesbia nuna*
Red-tailed Comet (left)	*Sappho sparganura*
Bronze-tailed Comet	*Polyonymus caroli*
Purple-backed Thornbill	*Ramphomicron microrhynchum*
Black-backed Thornbill	*Ramphomicron dorsale*
Bearded Mountaineer	*Oreonympha nobilis*
Bearded Helmetcrest	*Oxypogon guerinii*
Tyrian Metaltail	*Metallura tyrianthina*
Perija Metaltail	*Metallura iracunda*
Scaled Metaltail	*Metallura aeneocauda*
Fire-throated Metaltail	*Metallura eupogon*
Coppery Metaltail	*Metallura theresiae*
Neblina Metaltail	*Metallura odomae*
Violet-throated Metaltail	*Metallura baroni*
Viridian Metaltail	*Metallura williami*
Black Metaltail	*Metallura phoebe*
Rufous-capped Thornbill	*Chalcostigma ruficeps*
Olivaceous Thornbill	*Chalcostigma olivaceum*
Blue-mantled Thornbill	*Chalcostigma stanleyi*
Bronze-tailed Thornbill	*Chalcostigma heteropogon*
Rainbow-bearded Thornbill	*Chalcostigma herrani*
Mountain Avocetbill	*Opisthoprora euryptera*
Grey-bellied Comet	*Taphrolesbia griseiventris*
Long-tailed Sylph	*Aglaiocercus kingi*
Violet-tailed Sylph	*Aglaiocercus coelestis*
Venezuelan Sylph	*Aglaiocercus berlepschi*
Hyacinth Visorbearer	*Augastes scutatus*
Hooded Visorbearer	*Augastes lumachella*
Wedge-billed Hummingbird	*Augastes geoffroyi*
Purple-crowned Fairy	*Heliothryx barroti*
Black-eared Fairy	*Heliothryx aurita*
Horned Sungem	*Heliactin bilopha*
Marvellous Spatuletail	*Loddigesia mirabilis*
Plain-capped Starthroat	*Heliomaster constantii*
Long-billed Starthroat	*Heliomaster longirostris*
Stripe-breasted Starthroat	*Heliomaster squamosus*
Blue-tufted Starthroat	*Heliomaster furcifer*
Oasis Hummingbird	*Rhodopis vesper*
Peruvian Sheartail	*Thaumastura cora*
Sparkling-tailed Woodstar	*Tilmatura dupontii*
Slender Sheartail	*Doricha enicura*
Mexican Sheartail	*Doricha eliza*
Bahama Woodstar	*Calliphlox evelynae*
Magenta-throated Woodstar	*Calliphlox bryantae*

Purple-throated Woodstar	*Calliphlox mitchellii*
Amethyst Woodstar	*Calliphlox amethystina*
Slender-tailed Woodstar	*Microstilbon burmeisteri*
Lucifer Hummingbird	*Calothorax lucifer*
Beautiful Hummingbird	*Calothorax pulcher*
Vervain Hummingbird	*Mellisuga minima*
Bee Hummingbird	*Mellisuga helenae*
Ruby-throated Hummingbird (right)	*Archilochus colubris*
Black-chinned Hummingbird	*Archilochus alexandri*
Anna's Hummingbird	*Calypte anna*
Costa's Hummingbird	*Calypte costae*
Bumblebee Hummingbird	*Atthis heloisa*
Wine-throated Hummingbird	*Atthis ellioti*
Calliope Hummingbird	*Stellula calliope*
Purple-collared Woodstar	*Myrtis fanny*
Chilean Woodstar	*Myrtis yarrellii*
Short-tailed Woodstar	*Myrmia micrura*
White-bellied Woodstar	*Chaetocercus mulsant*
Little Woodstar	*Chaetocercus bombus*
Gorgeted Woodstar	*Chaetocercus heliodor*
Santa marta Woodstar	*Chaetocercus astreans*
Esmeraldas Woodstar	*Chaetocercus berlepschi*
Rufous-shafted Woodstar	*Chaetocercus jourdanii*
Volcano Hummingbird	*Selasphorus flammula*
Scintillant Hummingbird	*Selasphorus scintilla*
Glow-throated Hummingbird	*Selasphorus ardens*
Broad-tailed Hummingbird	*Selasphorus platycercus*
Rufous Hummingbird	*Selasphorus rufus*
Allen's Hummingbird	*Selasphorus sasin*

Left: **A Long-tailed Hermit (*Phaethornis superciliosus*) feeding at and pollinating passion flowers (*Passiflora vitifolia*) in Costa Rica.**

Hummingbird Hotspots

Arizona

Arizona-Sonora Desert Museum, Tucson.
Beatty's Apiary & Orchard, Miller Canyon.
Cave Creek Canyon, Portal.
Ramsey Canyon Mile-Hi Nature Conservation Preserve.
Santa Rita Lodge, Madera Canyon.
Southeastern Arizona Bird Observatory, Bisbee.
Wally & Marion Paton's House, Patagonia.

Texas

Rockport.
Fulton.

Trinidad

Asa Wright Nature Center.

Costa Rica

Rara Avis Reserve.
La Selva Biological Station.

Above: **A Green Violet-ear (*Colibri thalassinus*) feeding on an epiphytic orchid (*Elleanthus sp.*) in a Peruvian rainforest.**

Useful Web Sites

<www.birdwatchers.com/debtips.html>
Very useful feeding and gardening tips to attract hummingbirds.

<www.donaldburger.com/hbindex.htm/>
Donald R. Burger's web page detailing how to attract hummingbirds in Houston, Texas.

<www.flex.net/~lonestar/hummingbird.htm/>
Hummingbird facts and gardening hints.

<www.hummerlady.com/>
Beth Kingsley Hawkins picture gallery and experiences of hummingbirds.

<www.humming-birds.com/>
Facts & figures about hummingbirds and gardening and feeding tips for attracting hummingbirds.

<www.hummingbird.org/>
The official web site for the Hummingbird Society.

Below: **A White-bearded Hermit *(Phaethornis hispidus)* about to feed her young.**

Above: **A male Green-crowned Brilliant *(Heliodoxa jacula)* about to leave its perch in the Monteverde Cloud Forest of Costa Rica.**

<www.hummingbirds.net/>
Tips on watching, studying, feeding, and gardening to attract North American hummingbirds.

<www.ianr.unl.edu/pubs/Wildlife/g1331.HTM#pfh>
Tips on how to attract hummingbirds to the backyard in Nebraska hosted by the University of Nebraska-Lincoln, Institute of Agricultural and Natural Resources.

<www.nmnh.si.edu/BIRDNET/index.html/>
The Ornithological Information Source of the Ornithological Council hosted by the National Museum of Natural History (Smithsonian Institution).

<www.projectwildlife.org/find-hummingbirds.htm/>
A good resource on dealing with sick and injured hummingbirds.

<www.sabo.org/hummers.htm/>
The official web site of the Southeastern Arizona Bird Club (SABO) dedicated to conservation, study, and education for the birds of south-east Arizona with a special interest in scientific study and banding of hummingbirds.

<www.tonytilford.com/>
The author's web site specializing in wildlife around the world.

Bibliography & Further Reading

A Hummingbird in my House: The Story of Squeak – Arnette Heidcamp – Crown Publishers, 1991

Creating a Hummingbird Garden: A Guide to Identifying Hummingbird Visitors – Marcus Schneck, 1994

Handbook of the Birds of the World, Vol. 5 – Josep del Hoyo et al – Lynx Editions, 1999

How to Attract Hummingbirds & Butterflies – John V. Dennis & Mathew Tekulsky – Ortho Books, 1991

Hummingbird Gardens – Nancy L Newfield & Barbara Nielsen

Hummingbirds – Andrew Cleave – Hamlyn, 1989

Hummingbirds – C. H. Greenewalt – Dover Publications Inc., 1991

Hummingbirds – John Gould – Wordsworth Editions, 1990

Hummingbirds – Scott Weidensaul – Gallery Books, 1991

Hummingbirds of the Caribbean – Tyrrell E.Q. & R.A. – Crown Publishers, 1990

Hummingbirds: A Portrait of the Animal World – Hal H. Wyss – TODTRI, 1999

Hummingbirds: Jewels in Flight – Connie Toops – Voyageur Press, 1992

Hummingbirds: Their Life and Behavior – Tyrrell E.Q. & R.A. – Crown Publishers, 1985

Ruby-throated Hummingbird Book – Robert Sargent – Stackpole Books

The Hummingbird Book – Lilian & Donald Stokes – Little, Brown & Co., 1989

The Hummingbird Garden – Mathew Tekulsky – Crown Publishers, 1990

The Life of the Hummingbird – Alexander F. Skutch – Octopus, 1974

The Way of the Hummingbird – Virginia C. Holmgren – Capra Press, 1986

Glossary

Altitudinal migration	Movement from one altitude to another usually dependent on weather conditions and food availability
Barbules	The hairy interlocking structures emanating from the feather barbs which form the vane of a feather.
Coracoid	A paired ventral bone of the pectoral girdle.
Coverts	The small feathers at the base of the wings and tail that cover the bases of the larger flight feathers.
Epiphytes	A non-parasitic plant which grows upon another plant.
Flight membrane	The main airfoil surfaces formed by the flight feathers on which actual flight depends.
Gorget	A distinctive patch of feathers between the bird's throat and breast.
Gular	The region around the throat.
Hawking	A hovering and chasing habit employed to catch aerial insects.
Iridescent	A shining and colorful appearance of certain feathers due to spectral interference and light scattering, which changes depending on the angle of view.
Lores	The region between the front of the eye and the bill.
Malar	The region on the side of the neck just below the bill and eye.
Melanin	The dark colored pigments often present in skin and feathers.
Montane	A mountainous region usually above 3000ft (900 meters).
Nape	The region where back of the neck meets the back of the head.
Nominate	A term applied to the recognized form of a species from which sub-species are thought to have derived.
Platelets	A minute flat disc of cells.
Primary feathers	The flight feathers on the outer joint of the wing corresponding with the human hand.
Primary forest	Original or virgin forest.
Rufous	Reddish-brown color.
Savanna	Open grassland usually scattered with bushes and trees.
Secondary feathers	The flight feathers on the inner wing corresponding with the human forearm.
Secondary forest	New forest growth where original or primary forest has been removed.

Left: **A female Green-backed Firecrown (*Sephanoides s.*) returning to her nest in Southern Chile.**

Page 160: **A Giant Hummingbird (*Patagona gigas*) settled down for the night.**

Index

Alberta 126, 120
Allen's Hummingbird *(Archilochus colubris)* 26, 142, 143
Alaska 140
Amazilia Hummingbird *(Amazilia amazilia)* 82, 83
Andean Hillstar *(Oreotrochilus estella)* 18, 26, 149
Andes 29, 34, 36, 42, 44, 56, 98, 106, 114
Anna's Hummingbird *(Calypte anna)* 21, 24, 29, 130, 131, 144
Argentina 62, 110, 112
Arizona 96, 130, 138
Arizona-Sonora Desert Museum, Tuscon 152
Aruba 52
Asa Wright Nature Center 152
Atacama Desert 110, 112, 122
Aztecs 8

Bahama Islands 64
Bananaquit *(Coereba flaveola)* 18, 58
barbules 14
Beatty's Apiary and Orchard, Miller canyon 152
Black-billed Streamertail *(Trochilus scitulus)* 58
Black-breasted Puffleg *(Eriocnemis nigrivestis)* 9
Black-chinned Hummingbird *(Archilochus alexandri)* 15, 24, 31, 128, 129
Black-crested Coquette *(Lophornis helenae)* 56
Black-throated Mango *(Anthracothorax nigricollis)* 48
Blue-chinned Sapphire *(Chlorostilbon notatus)* 60, 61
Blue-headed Hummingbird *(Cyanophaia bicolor)* 72, 73
Blue-throated Hummingbird *(Lampornis clemenciae)* 92, 93
Blue-tufted Starthroat *(Heliomaster furcifer)* 120, 121
Bolivia 48, 52, 108, 114, 118
Booted Raquet-tail *(Ocreatus underwoodii)* 116, 117
Broad-billed Hummingbird *(Cyanthus latirostris)* 20, 21, 70, 71, 147
Broad-tailed Hummingbird *(Selasphorus platycercus)* 13, 29, 138, 139
Buenos Aires 78
Buff-tailed Sicklebill *(Eutoxeres condamini)* 32

California 128, 130, 142
Callaque volcanoes 118
Calliope Hummingbird *(Stellula calliope)* 28, 31, 134, 135
Cave Creek Canyon Mile-Hi Nature Conseravation Preserve 152
Chihuahua 92
Chile 110, 114, 122
Cinnamon Hummingbird *(Amazilia rutila)* 84, 85
Collared Inca *(Coeligena torquata)* 106, 107
Columbia 32, 38, 46, 108
Coppery-headed Emerald *(Elvira cupreiceps)* 67
Costa Rica 28, 32, 40–42, 44, 66, 67, 74, 94, 102, 124, 134
Costa's Hummingbird *(Calypte costae)* 132, 133
Cuban Emerald *(Chlorostilbon ricordii)* 64, 146

Dominica 72

Ecquador 57, 80, 82, 100, 106, 114
Escudo de Veraguas 80

Fawn-breasted Brilliant *(Heliodoxa rubinoides)* 98, 99
Fiery-throated Hummingbird *(Panterpe insignis)* 66
Fork-tailed Woodnymph *(Thalurania furcata)* 76, 77
French Guiana 39, 48, 54, 60
Frilled Coquette *(Lophornis magnificus)* 27, 54, 55

Giant Hummingbird *(Patagona gigas)* 2, 15, 110, 111, 149, 159
Glittering-bellied Emerald *(Chlorostilbon aureoventris)* 62, 63
Goias 120
Gondwanaland 10
Goyaz 42
Green Hermit *(Phaethronis guy)* 36, 37
Green Mango *(Anthracothorax viridis)* 15, 49, 146
Green Violet-ear *(Colibri thalassinus)* 11, 44, 45, 152
Green-backed Firecrown *(Sephanoides s.)* 17, 23, 24, 27, 112, 113, 157
Green-crowned Brilliant *(Heliodoxa jacula)* 100, 101, 154
Green-fronted Lancebill *(Doryfera ludovicae)* 40
Greenish Puffleg *(Haplophaedia aureliae)* 115, 150
Grenada 34
Guatemala 41, 56, 74, 84, 96, 138
Gulf of Mexico 29, 126, 128

Hairy Hermit *(Glaucis hirsuta)* 34, 35
Hondura Emerald *(Polyerata luciae)* 9
Honduras 74, 90, 96
Hook billed Hermit *(Glaucis dohmii)* 8
humerus 10

Incas 8
Isle of Pines 64

Jamaica 50, 58
Jamaican Mango *(Anthracothorax mango)* 50, 51
Juan Fernandez Firecrown *(Sephaniodes fernandensis)* 9, 114

Lake Maracaibo 106
Lake Titicaca 104
La Selva Biological Station 152
Las Tres Marias 84
leks 23, 25
Long-tailed Hummingbird *(Phaethornis superciliosus)* 151

Magenta-throated Woodstar *(Calliphox bryantae)* 124, 125
Magnificent Hummingbird *(Eugenes fulgens)* 102, 103
Maranhao 42
Martinique 72
Marvelous Spatuletail *(Loddigesia mirabilis)* 14
Matto Grasso 42, 55, 120
Mayan 8
Mexico 41, 42, 68, 86, 92, 102, 132
Monteverde Cloud Forest 154
Musuem of National History (Smithsonian Institute) 154

Nayarit 70, 84
nectar 16-19
Nicaragua 42, 44, 56, 74, 84, 90, 94, 96
Nova Scotia 126

Oasis Hummingbird *(Rhodopsis vesper)* 122, 123
Oregon 142

Panama 40, 66, 90, 94, 100, 124, 134
Penambuco 78
Peru 6, 8, 34, 46, 48, 98, 106, 108
Phaethornithae 144
platelets 14
Puerto Rican Emerald *(Chlorostilbon maugaeus)* 65
Purple-crowned Woodnymph *(Thalurania columbica venusta)* 6
Purple-crowned Woodnymph *(Thalurania columbica)* 74, 75
Purple-throated Carib *(Eulampis jugularis)* 14
Purple-throated Mountain Gem *(Lampornis castaneoventris cololaema)* 11

Rara Avis Reserve 153
Red-billed Streamertail *(Trochilus polymus)* 58, 59
Reddish Hermit *(Phaethornis ruber)* 39
Red-tailed Comet *(Sappho sparganura)* 118, 119, 150
Rio Grande 120
River Trombetas 60
Rocky Mountains 134
Ruby-Topaz Hummingbird *(Chrysolampis mosquitus)* 6, 52, 53

Ruby-throated Hummingbird (*Archilochus colubris*) 18, 26, 29, 126, 127, 151
Rufous Hummingbird (*Selasphorus rufus*) 25, 140, 141, 147
Rufous-tailed Hummingbird (*Amazilia tzacatl*) 80, 81

San Luis Potosi 70
San Salvador 55
Santa Catarina 55
Santa Rita Lodge, Madera Canyon 152
Sao Paulo 78
Sapphire-bellied Hummingbird (*Lepidopyga lillae*) 9
Scintillant Hummingbird (*Selasphorus scintilla*) 136, 137
Scissor-tailed Hummingbird (*Hylonympha macrocerca*) 9
Shining Sunbeam (*Aglaectis cupripennis*) 104, 105
Sierra Nevada 134
Snowcap (*Microchera albocoronata*) 90, 91, 148
Sonora 92
Southeasterm Arizona Bird Club (SABO) 154
Southeastern Arizona Bird Observatory 30, 152
Southern Chipas 41
Sparkling Violet-ear (*Colibri coruscans*) 27, 44, 45, 152
Steely-vented Hummingbird (*Saucerrottei saucerrottei*) 88, 89
Stripe-tailled Hummingbird (*Eupherusa axima*) 68, 69
swifts (*Apodidae*) 10
Sword-billed Hummingbird (*Ensifera ensifera*) 18, 108, 109

Tamaulipas 70
Texas 96, 132, 138, 140
Tobago 34, 52, 60
Treeswifts (*Hemiprocnidae*) 10
Trinidad 34, 36, 42, 52
Trochilidae 28, 144
Tufted Coquette (*Lophornis ornatus*) 54
Turquiose-throated Puffleg (*Eriocnemis godini*) 9

Universty of Nebraska-Lincoln 154
Uraguay 62
Utah 138

Variable Mountain Gem (*Lampornis castneoventris*) 94, 95
Venezuela 34, 36, 38, 44, 54, 60, 74, 88, 114
Vera Cruz 56, 68
Villarica volcanoes 118
Violet Sabrewing (*Campylopterus hemileucurus*) 41
Violet-crowned Hummingbird (*Agyrtria violoceps*) 86, 87

Washington Convention of International Trade in Endangered Species (CITES) 8
White-bearded Hummingbird (*Phaethornis hispidus*) 25, 38, 153
White-chinned Sapphire (*Hylocharis cyanus*) 78, 79
White-eared Hummingbird (*Basilima leucotis*) 96, 97, 148
White-necked Jacobin (*Florisuga mellivora*) 42, 43
White-throated Mountain Gem (*Lampornis c. castaneoventris*) 17
White-tipped Sicklebill (*Eutoxeres aquila*) 32, 33
Williamson, Sheri 30
Wire-crested Thorntail (*Discosura popelairii*) 57
Wyoming 138

Photographic Credits

The publisher wishes to thank the following for kindly supplying the photography for this book:

(For front and back covers, see inside flaps.)

Pages: 2, 16(left), 17(top), 18(top), 19(bottom), 23, 24(top), 25(middle & bottom), 26(bottom right), 27(bottom), 35, 38, 39, 47, 77, 79, 105, 109, 110, 111, 113, 119, 121, 123, 133(inset), 144, 149(both), 150(left), 153, 156, 160 courtesy of © Günter Ziesler

Pages: 5(top left, bottom left, top right), 7, 8, 18(bottom), 20(left), 27(top & middle), 53, 55, 57, 63, 73, 83, 99, 117 courtesy of © Tony Tilford

Pages: 5(bottom right), 28, 130, 135 courtesy of © TC Nature, 1998, 131, 145 courtesy of © 1996 TC NATURE

Pages: 6, 11, 12, 40, 41, 56, 66, 95(bottom), 125, 151(bottom), 152, 154 courtesy of © Michael & Patricia Fogden

Pages: 9, 33, 85, 107 courtesy of © Kevin Schafer/CORBIS

Pages: 13, 139 courtesy of © D. Robert Franz/CORBIS

Pages: 14, 15(both), 21(left), 26(bottom middle), 141, 142, 143 courtesy of © George Lepp/CORBIS

Pages: 16(right), 17(bottom), 20(right), 45, 49, 64, 65, 75, 87, 91, 95(top), 97, 101, 115, 146(both), 148(both), 150(right) courtesy of © Greg W. Lasley

Pages: 16(middle), 24(left bottom & right bottom), 43, 48, 51, 59, 61, 81, 103, 138 courtesy of © Beth Kingsley Hawkins

Page: 19(top) courtesy of © Lynda Richardson/CORBIS

Pages: 21(right), 22, 29, 70, 147(top) courtesy of © Joe McDonald/CORBIS

Pages: 25(top), 26 (bottom left) courtesy of © Ron Austing: Frank Lane Picture Agency/CORBIS

Page: 26(top) courtesy of © W. Wayne Lockwood, M.D./CORBIS

Pages: 30 courtesy of © 1995 Tom Wood, 31(bottom left) courtesy of © 1997 Tom Wood

Page: 31(top) courtesy of © 1997 SABO (volunteer photo)

Page: 31(bottom right) courtesy of ©1997 Sheri Williamson

Page: 37 courtesy of © Picture Press/CORBIS

Page: 54 courtesy of © Wolfgang Kaehler/CORBIS

Pages: 67, 69, 89, 137 courtesy of © Michael & Patricia Fogden/CORBIS

Pages: 71, 127, 128, 129, 140 courtesy of © Pictor International - London

Pages: 80, 147(bottom) courtesy of © Steve Kaufman/CORBIS

Page: 92 courtesy of © Terry Whittaker: Frank Lane Picture Agency/CORBIS

Page 93: courtesy of © Tim Zurowski/CORBIS

Page 102: courtesy of © Eric and David Hosking/CORBIS

Page 114: courtesy of © John Francis/CORBIS

Pages: 126, 151(top) courtesy of © Richard Hamilton Smith/CORBIS

Page: 133(main) courtesy of © Ralph A. Clevenger/CORBIS